NO TIME TO LOSE

To Bill's courageous mother,
with gratitude, admiration
and respect.

A.P.

NO TIME TO LOSE

The fast-moving world of Bill Ivy

by

Alan Peck

MRP

MOTOR RACING PUBLICATIONS LTD
Unit 6, The Pilton Estate, 46 Pitlake, Croydon CR0 3RY

First published 1972
This edition 1997

British Library Cataloguing in Publication Data

Peck, Alan
No time to lose : the fast moving world of Bill Ivy. - 2nd ed.
1. Ivy, Bill 2. Motorcyclists - Biography 3. Motorcycle racing
I. Title
796.7'5'092

ISBN 1 899870 21 0

This book has been set in 11 pt Imprint.
Printed and bound in Great Britain by
Hartnolls Ltd, Bodmin, Cornwall

Chapters

Acknowledgments

IT IS A MEASURE of Bill Ivy's universal popularity that I received so much enthusiastic encouragement and assistance when I let it be known that I was compiling data for a manuscript in his memory. To everyone who helped me in this way, whether they provided words, pictures, memories or advice – and in some cases it was all of these – may I record my deepest gratitude.

Many of those who assisted me are mentioned on the pages which follow, but many more are not, which does not mean that their help was valued any the less; they were, alas, victims of the painful task of reducing 350,000 words of notes and countless yards of tape to a suitable-length typescript.

The staff of *Motor Cycle, Motor Cycle News* and *Motor* were most generous in their efforts to fill the gaps in Mrs Ivy's personal photographic record of her son's all-too-brief career, and I am indebted to the following individual photographers whose work has helped to illustrate this book: David Dixon, Gordon Francis, Jim Greening, Jan Heese, Brian Holder, Tom March, C. V. Middleton, Dr. Benno Müller, F. B. Scott, Jaroslav Sejk, John Stoddart and Leslie Thacker. I wish I could add to this list the names of others who, either by accident or design, submitted photographs anonymously, either to Mrs Ivy or to myself, and who collectively have provided several of the selected pictures.

Determined as I was to pay a personal tribute to a great sportsman, I would have failed had it not been for the support and encouragement I received from so many sources, and if this book is worthy of Bill Ivy's memory it is due in large measure to the efforts of those stalwarts whom I pestered so much, yet whose doors were never closed on me. Thank you all for being so patient!

A.P.

Foreword

by the late Mike Hailwood GM, BEM

WHEN BILL IVY was killed at the East German Grand Prix motorcycle sport suffered an immeasurable loss for he, in my view, was the last of the great characters.

And it would, therefore, have been a sad commentary on our appreciation of his skills and his bravery had somebody not taken the steps to give a lasting tribute to the wee fellow.

I am happy to be associated with this account of his racy attitude to life and to the sport and to be able to endorse the thoughts of millions of enthusiasts all over the world who were both thrilled and chilled by Bill's determined style.

We were friends – close pals in fact – despite the fact that professionally we represented different works and, on the circuits, had to be the deadliest of rivals.

The racing rivalry, with hard-fought contests every outing, never impinged on our association as two bachelors hell bent on getting the best out of life when the races were over and done with.

He was a way-out character, anxious to be involved in whatever was fashionable at the time, and that meant long flowing hair and flared trousers, with garish shirts and a blinding line in neckwear.

His taste in sports cars, too, was eye-catching and you could always tell when he had turned up at the circuit by the screeching of tortured tyres on the tarmac or gravel and the pluming dust-storm that seemed to be his trademark of every spectacular arrival.

He could walk on his hands for miles and was a man of immense strength in those forearms and shoulders. But despite his lack of stature he had no fear, and he showed that – and his strength, too – by clouting a Belgian policeman who tried to push him around outside the circuit at Spa!

He was a cheeky little rogue and, in many ways, the little man trying to look bigger. That's why, I suppose, his car always had to be the flashiest around.

But when he was out on that wriggling ribbon of road, pitting his wits and talents against the rest of us, he was as tall as any man in the world.

His TT performances are legend, and his utter contempt for the hazards that its 37¾ miles could bring him showed me, at least, that there was not a braver man in a game that breeds bravery.

Had he lived I have no doubt that World Championship titles would have come easily to him, for he was reaching a stage of development that made him a tough man to get past.

The years I knew him, the races we had, and the times we spent together in the world's nightclubs, with Bill demanding steak and chips wherever he went – even in Japan – are precious to me as memories of what was one of the most enjoyable passages of my own life.

His body was a criss-cross of stitch marks from some fearsome crashes but, even though he lived on the limit, he never backed off a single challenge. I would not say he was fearless – no man is that – but I would offer the opinion that his margins of safety were narrower than most, and his ability to take advantage of that state of affairs was well-known by many riders who tried to follow him.

The sad thing about his death is that the world of racing never really saw the best of Bill Ivy. But I hope we don't forget what we did see . . . a giant of a little man.

Mike Hailwood was fatally injured in a road accident at Portway, the Midlands, March 1981.

I

Born mobile

SUE IVY'S journey to work was no different from anyone else's; it was just an ordinary bus ride, at least it was until her younger brother, Bill, reached his sixteenth birthday and bought himself a motorbike. After that, her journey became something of a nightmare. The trouble was that Bill took the same route as the bus, and from the very first day he had the motorbike he would speed past it at a terrific rate, to either the amusement, the annoyance or the sheer terror of the passengers. It became a regular feature of the bus journey to watch Bill blast past at speed, hooting and waving, and the passengers were soon predicting confidently that the 'young hooligan' would wrap himself around a tree before the week was up. Little did they know that the tearaway's sister was sitting amongst them!

Sue would sit in her seat, dreading the moment when Bill would speed past on his 'command performance', which became the highlight of an otherwise dull journey for the other occupants. When she heard shouts of 'Here he comes again . . .', 'Mad as a hatter . . .', and 'Bloody little fool . . .', Sue would shrink down in her seat, trying to look unconcerned and adopting an air of indifference. Of course she told her brother about the stir he was creating among the people on the bus, but instead of having the desired effect of slowing him down it goaded him into going even faster. Whenever he saw the green Maidstone and District vehicle in the distance, Bill knew that he had an audience, and it made him show off all the more, much to Sue's annoyance.

This incident is one of many so typical of Bill Ivy. It serves to illustrate, not only his love of speed, but also his character, for he was a real showman, even at the age of 16. In later years he thrilled race crowds the world over with his brilliant riding, which hoisted him among the élite at the very top of motorcycle road racing.

He also became extremely popular with his contemporaries, a larger-than-life figure with a flamboyant personality. Some of his antics offended a small minority, the type of people who can accept nothing even remotely unconventional, but it was Ivy's character, as much as his riding ability, which endeared him to thousands.

They say that World Champions are born, rather than made, and this was certainly true in little Bill's case, for he was born on the move, in an ambulance on the way to hospital. On August 27, 1942 an ambulance carrying Mrs Nell Ivy to Pembury Hospital, from her home near Maidstone, in Kent, lost its way, and before the vehicle reached its destination Mrs Ivy had delivered a son, later christened William David. Many years later, when Ivy began to climb the ladder of success and he was asked, 'How did you first become interested in a life of speed?', he replied, 'Fate destined me to it; right from birth I was in a hurry!'

As Bill grew up, this early addiction for speed grew with him, and even at the age of three-and-a-half that tigerish attitude was beginning to form, for the little boy discovered that he could clamber on his sister's pushbike with the aid of a soapbox. Later, some of his primary school escapades convinced Mrs Ivy that her son was quite a scatterbrain. He skinned his bottom in roller-skating incidents, and on one occasion took the skin off his hands and face in a tumble on his cycle. This occurred on a steep winding hill near the Ivys' home. Bill would dash down the hill, challenging himself not to use the brakes, and eventually he had it down to a fine art; it was no problem at all for him, until the time heavy overnight rain washed gravel on to one of the corners. Bill came charging down, completely ignoring the brakes as usual, cranked over into the bend and then hit the loose surface with disastrous results. Extensive gravel-rash kept him in bed for a week, bandaged like an Egyptian mummy, but it didn't discourage him.

One of the annual photographs taken at Sutton Valence Primary School around 1950 shows the governors, headmaster, teachers, and catering staff in the back row, with all the pupils lined up in regimental formation at the front. Right in the centre of the front row, sitting cross-legged on the grass, with his tongue lolling out and pulling a hideous face, is William David Ivy. He was severely told-off for spoiling the whole scene, but this was probably when his fame first began to spread, for one can imagine proud children bearing home copies of the school photograph, and their parents immediately asking, 'Who on *earth* is that boy in the front row?'

Ivy's schooldays followed the pattern of most other youngsters.

After his primary school education he was transferred to Old Borough Manor School, in the tiny village of Loose on the outskirts of Maidstone. Although he tried hard academically, Bill was a middle-stream boy of average ability, but he excelled in the practical subjects, was good with his hands and noted for his skill in sporting activities, particularly gymnastics. He once dressed up in a chimp suit and provided great entertainment by bounding about and mimicking the antics of a chimpanzee at one of the school shows.

Mr Cocksedge, the woodwork master, remembers when Ivy first went to the school:

'He was one of the smallest boys we had. In his first year he hardly came up to the level of the woodwork benches – and what a mischievous little blighter he was, too! Never vicious or abusive, he had a nice sort of naughtiness about him. He never played devilish tricks; he was a happy, lively lad, with a jolly good sense of humour coupled with an air of impish cheek. One couldn't help but like him. One day I found it necessary to curb his exuberance by whacking him across the backside with a dowel-rod, but he never bore a grudge, or sulked, as some boys do when they get on the wrong side of a teacher. In no time at all he would come bouncing back at you, rather like an 'India-rubber' boy.'

Another teacher who had the task of educating Bill in her form for a year was Mrs Colegate. One incident sticks vividly in her mind:

'Every year, the teachers put on a Christmas concert for the pupils, and in this particular show I was wrapped up in a blanket, right up to my chin. We were acting an execution scene, and at the end of the act I had to cast the blanket off, pleading, "Don't shoot me – I'm a woman!", and exposing myself as a very scantily clad harem girl. The young audience gasped, then applauded enthusiastically – they had never seen a lady teacher so briefly clothed. The next morning I walked into my classroom, and there was a buzz of conversation regarding my previous evening's performance. Little Billy came up, gave me a nudge and a saucy wink. "Cor. . . . Miss. . . . corrrr . . .!", was his only comment, but the look in his eyes spoke volumes – and he was only 11 years old! His interest in the opposite sex was already very apparent.

'If there was something to laugh at, or if anything could be twisted to make it amusing, Billy would always be in the thick of it.

He would pull a teacher's leg in a gentle sort of way, but his manners were impeccable.'

On the school sports day, a slow-cycle 'race' was included in the activities. The idea is for all contestants to ride with their feet up over a measured distance; anyone putting either foot on the ground is eliminated, and the last one to cross the finishing line is the winner. The astonishing thing was that Bill would only move about a yard in the time it took the others to overbalance, put their feet down, or complete the course, so good was his sense of balance.

An early example of his ingenuity was the cycle he rode at the age of 11. It had telescopic front forks and swinging-arm rear suspension, 'knobbly' dirt track tyres, and speedway-type handlebars. Although Mr Ivy helped modify the cycle, it was Bill's idea, and that bike was the envy of all the other lads. Bill spent hours practising broadsiding and balancing round the allotments near his home.

It was only a matter of time before he realised that cycles had their limitations, and he started pestering his father for a motorbike, so a Francis-Barnett two-stroke was bought. Mr and Mrs Ivy were grass-track racing enthusiasts, and they often attended meetings at weekends, taking the whole family with them. When Bill got his motorbike he put his spectating to good use by flying round the paths on the allotment, trying to emulate the heroes of the dirt. Some of the other boys tried to make things more difficult for him by throwing buckets of water over the corners, making the grass very slippery, and this practice caught out Bill many times. Often he would lose control and plough through a bean row or cast himself off in a cabbage patch to the considerable dismay of the gardeners, who were not amused to find their vegetables reduced to a load of pulp by a cork-brained 'earwig' on a motorcycle, after they had lavished so much care and attention upon them. So the irate 'greenfingers' men contacted the police, and young William was forcibly ejected, with stern warnings of the consequences if he was caught riding on the ground again.

Silence reigned over the allotments once more, and the gardeners went back to work, happy in the knowledge that their vegetables were safe, but ignorant of the fact that they had witnessed the early efforts of a small boy who was destined to conquer the world of two wheels.

Roy Francis was Bill's best school-chum, and his father had a farm, so when Bill was turned off the allotments and had nowhere to ride Roy asked his father if they could ride round one of the fields. Mr Francis said 'Yes', and the machine was duly transported to the farm, and from then on the two boys almost lived on that old bike. Most evenings and every weekend the Barnett's exhaust would echo across the Kentish countryside, and other boys came along, too, attracted by the thrill of thrashing round a field on two wheels. A course was mapped out, and the boys would time each other to see who could lap the fastest. Bill was the smallest of the gang and when he sat on the bike his feet hardly touched the ground, but he was the fastest for none of the others could match his pluck and determination.

After a while, Bill wanted something more powerful, so he sold the Barnett to Roy and bought a 350cc Triumph Tiger 80. Things were much more exciting with two machines in the stable, for the lads were able to race against each other, although often there would be only one bike in commission at a time as the other would be in pieces. Considering the hammering to which they were subjected, the machines stood up to it very well, especially as they were being used for purposes which the makers never intended. But the boys soon had to learn about the mechanical side of things to keep them going, and every spare penny was pooled and spent on petrol or spare parts. But it was money well spent, for it gave the boys hours of fun, taught them how to ride away from the dangers of public roads, and gave them a basic knowledge of engines, and as far as their parents were concerned, it kept them off the streets and out of mischief.

Bill had formed his ambition to be a motorcycle mechanic long before leaving school, and he also had a strong desire to enter grass-track racing when he was old enough. At this stage of his life, road racing didn't really interest him.

Mr Ivy was a boxing fan – he'd done a bit himself in his youth – and when the opportunity to learn the noble art arose at Old Borough Manor, he urged young Bill into donning the gloves. Although he was very light, and lacked inches in height and reach (a distinct disadvantage in the fight game) Bill lacked nothing in pluck. He won 11 of the 12 bouts that he contested, despite boxing over his weight most of the time. It was a major problem finding suitable opponents for Ivy because he was so small, and frequently he found himself facing a boy who was not only bigger, but also considerably heavier. However, the little fellow fought his way through to the Kent Schoolboy Finals, and only lost on points. This was his last fight in the ring. He never really enjoyed boxing, and had come to regard it as 'a mug's game'; he couldn't see the point of two people going into a ring just to knock each other about. But tiny though he was, Bill was never picked on by the school bullies; those types never have a go at people who can look after themselves.

On leaving school at the age of 15, Bill wanted to go straight into one of the local motorcycle shops, but his parents wanted him to take a job where he could be properly apprenticed and achieve the necessary qualifications. A letter was sent to the AMC factory near Woolwich, where the legendary AJS, Matchless, and Manx Norton racing machines were manufactured, asking if they had a vacancy in their competition department. An interview was arranged, and Bill, accompanied by his mother, travelled up to the famous Plumstead factory to see what could be done.

The gentleman who conducted the interview must have found it hard to believe that the small boy confronting him (who looked far younger than his 15 years) had really left school and wanted a job. His surprise turned to astonishment when Bill calmly told him that he rode a big Triumph round a field. Turning his quizzical expression to Mrs Ivy, the gentleman obviously doubted the truth in this statement. 'Yes, that's correct,' she told him. This must have helped towards creating a good impression for Bill got the job.

The job itself wasn't quite what Bill expected. He assumed that he would be put straight on to the task of working on engines, but as anyone who has served an apprenticeship knows, the first few months are usually spent running errands or sweeping up. Poor Bill, he desperately wanted to work on the bikes, and could even pull half of his own machine to pieces and rebuild it, but there he was at AMC's pushing a broom round the factory floor most of the time. During his first two weeks there he didn't lay a spanner on a solitary nut, and this disillusioned him. He thought that at the rate things were going it would be months before he would even be allowed to screw in a sparking plug. Also, the factory was a long way from home, which posed rather a travelling problem, so Bill asked his mother if she could contact Chisholm's, the Maidstone dealers, on his behalf to see if they could give him a job. Mrs Ivy rang them, they said 'Yes', so Bill left the AMC factory on the Friday and started at Chisholm's the following Monday. Undoubtedly, this was the decision that first set Bill Ivy on the path to fame.

The Chisholm brothers, Bill and Don, were partners in the motorcycle business. They knew Bill's father well, but young Bill they knew only by reputation, and when the little chap turned up for work that first morning, they were surprised to find out just how small he was. Bill Chisholm remembers vividly Ivy's early days at the shop:

'In those days we had a long counter which segregated the shop from the workshops behind. There was an opening in the counter with a hinged flap on the top, and Billy was so tiny that he could walk right through it when the flap was down, just by ducking his head.

'From the very beginning it was obvious that he knew quite a lot about motorcycles. He was a bright, keen-eyed boy. His eyes would be darting everywhere taking in everything, and he would almost anticipate what you wanted. He was a very quick learner.'

Don Chisholm can even remember the first job he gave Bill to do:

'We had an old 250cc Royal Enfield which somebody else had stripped down. It was a bit of a rough old bike, and I thought I'd better give him something to do just to get him initiated, so I said, "Do you think you can do anything with that, Bill?" He said that he would have a go at it, and he built the whole engine up himself with advice from us. It was obvious that he knew what he was doing.'

So Bill settled into his new job. He had taken the first step towards achieving part of his ambition, but he would have to wait almost a year before he could do anything about wanting to race; driving and competition licences were not issued to anyone under the age of 16, no matter how keen they were. Impatient for his next birthday to arrive, Bill had to content himself with riding round the field on the Triumph, which by now he had considerably modified. He had converted the rigid frame to swinging-arm rear suspension, and the whole bike was virtually rebuilt to dirt track specification.

Several members of the Maidstone Aces Motorcycle Club often got together to hold an afternoon's unofficial racing amongst themselves on private land, and Bill went along one day; despite getting a puncture in his rear tyre mid-way through the proceedings he won every race except one, when he fell off and remounted to finish second. And he competed in half the events with a flat tyre! The opposition included several experienced motorcyclists, so Bill's performances impressed everyone.

At about this time Dave Swift, who later became Bill's brother-in-law, started dating Sue, and he will never forget the first time he met his girlfriend's younger brother. On his first visit to the Ivy home Sue took him out into the garage, swung the door open and said, 'This is my little brother, Bill.' Dave walked inside, and there, crouched on the floor, covered in grime and oil smuts was a scruffy little object working on a motorcycle. Dave's first reaction was, 'My God, what on earth have we got here?'.

Young brothers are well-known for being a hindrance to their big sisters' courting activities on the sofa, and Bill was no different from any other kid-brother in this respect. Dave, in moments of exasperation, soon learnt that the only way to get rid of him was to tell him to clear off and go for a ride on his motorbike, so Bill, unknown to his parents, would jump on Dave's machine and tear off for a ride round the network of quiet country lanes around Maidstone. The fact that he was neither insured, nor old enough to ride on the public roads, didn't worry him in the least, and quite oblivious of the fact that he had ruined Sue and Dave's evening anyway (because as soon as he departed, they were confronted by a nagging concern, lest the little terror came to some harm or was caught by the Law) Bill sped along to his heart's content, revelling in the new thrill of racing along on metalled roads.

At last the long-awaited day arrived when Ivy reached his 16th birthday. It opened up whole new horizons; testing customers' machines at the shop, going off on errands to collect spare parts instead of being confined to the workshop and the odd walk down the road, and no longer did he have to steal a few cherished outings on Dave's bike. Now Bill could ride where and when he liked, legitimately, and he thoroughly enjoyed his new-found freedom.

A 500cc sprung-hub Triumph Speed Twin was the first machine that Bill purchased, and with it he soon gained the respect of the older, more experienced riders who congregated in the various cafés around Maidstone. Nobody could stay with the eight-stone, five-foot, wisp of a boy who threw his big Triumph through bends with such verve and skill, and customers who took their mounts to Chisholm's for repairs could scarcely believe their ears, or their eyes, when Bill was told to take their bike out for a spin to see if it had been repaired satisfactorily.

Motorcyclists are notorious for their fastidious dedication to their machines. They fuss over them, polish them until they gleam, and are most reluctant about letting other people ride them, least of all a half-pint lad who didn't look old enough to ride a moped let alone a 650!

The others who worked at the shop used to enjoy watching the

Bill Ivy, Marks 1, 2 and 3. *Above:* At school; this time he kept his tongue in! *Above right:* A still-youthful King of Brands celebrates his victory. *Right:* Long-haired and trendy, 1968-style.

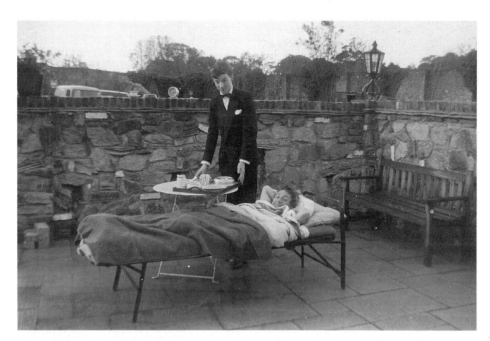

Above: Taking it easy; breakfast in bed on the hotel patio preceded an endurance ride at Goodwood. *Below:* Working hard; a spectator, watching Ivy wrestling with the big 750cc Matchless, remarked that it was like seeing a dog shaking a rat!

Above: Bill on the Monard leading Griff Jenkins and a sliding Dave Croxford at Druids Hill Bend, Brands Hatch, during an Unlimited race. *Right:* Scrapping with Dave Degens at Mallory Park; Bill went on to another win on the 500cc Kirby-Matchless.

Above: Formation at Brands Hatch. Bill leads Paddy Driver (Kirby-AJS) and Derek Minter (Petty-Norton) on Geoff Monty's 350cc Norton; Ivy was about to leave Monty and join Tom Kirby's team. *Left:* Romping away with the 125cc race at the 1965 Mallory Park post-TT meeting on the Chis-Honda. *Above right:* Mike Hailwood said that Bill fell over about 90 times the first time he went skiing! *Right:* At Brands Hatch on a 50cc Honda.

Left: The big moment. Bill has just become the British 500cc Chamption after a hectic struggle with Derek Minter at Oulton Park; but the smile disappeared when he returned to the paddock a few minutes later ... *Above:* Bill at Brands on the 500cc Kirby/Rickman Metisse; this machine was successful from the start, but the 350cc version twice landed Bill in hospital through oil problems.

The Mutawakelite Kingdom of Yemen honoured motorcycle racing with a series of 'Champions of Sport' postage stamps. Bill Ivy, Giacomo Agostini, Phil Read and Kel Carruthers were familiar names but Hail Wood was a newcomer, though he did look remarkably like Mike!

look of anguish tempered by sheer disbelief on the faces of customers as Bill wheeled their machine out on to the pavement. There
he would turn on the petrol and adjust the air and ignition levers
as the customer looked on dubiously – a mute, reluctant audience.
'He'll never start it!', was the smug thought as the little figure
swung down the kick-start with all his might. But invariably the
engine would burst into life first time, and with a cheery 'Shan't
be a tick', Ivy would charge off with the motor revving and
exhausts bellowing, leaving the anxious owner standing in a cloud
of smoke, by now convinced that his beautiful steed was destined
for a terrible fate in the inexperienced hands of a small boy. After a
few minutes Bill would come flying back, and the relieved customer
would beam all over his face when told 'She's going like a bomb',
and heap praise on Bill for his handling of such a big bike; in the
end everyone would enjoy a good laugh.

Regular customers at the shop, and people living in the vicinity,
soon became used to the sight of an apparently riderless motorcycle
hurtling towards them, which, on closer inspection revealed a tiny
jockey at the controls, flat on the tank in typical racing style. But
being small did have its disadvantages when stopping, for Bill still
wasn't big enough to put both feet on the ground whilst sitting
astride most bikes, and he was often in danger of overbalancing
whilst stationary. He found the answer to this problem by adopting
the habit of flicking the prop-stand out with his foot immediately
before stopping. One day, he came careering into one of the café
forecourts, attempted to hook the prop-stand out, missed it, and
fell off in an ungainly heap in front of the whole gang. All the
others thought it was hilarious that Bill, the best rider among
them, had great difficulty in staying on his bike when he wasn't
actually moving!

He was so keen on riding that he never missed an opportunity of
taking a bike out for a spin at the shop. On one occasion, Don asked
him to pop down the road for something, and Bill's eyes lit up.
'Can I take a bike?' he asked.

'Take a bike!' Don replied, 'It's only just down the road – what
do you think your feet are for?'

With typical impishness, Bill held up his right foot and said,
'This one is for changing gear. . . ,' then holding up his other foot,
'and this one is for stamping on the brake!'

Don burst out laughing. 'Go on, you cheeky young devil . . . take
a bike and clear off.' The Chisholm brothers have never forgotten
that classic Ivy remark.

B

Most motorcyclists gain some of their experience the hard way, and it was inevitable that Bill should have his share of incidents. One evening, whilst returning home from work, he discovered that some drivers do stupid, unpredictable things. Motoring along in his usual position – flat on the tank – he was suddenly confronted by a large lorry reversing into the road without supervision. Unable to avoid the obstruction, Bill crashed heavily and was carted off to hospital. It was two days before he regained consciousness, and when Mr Ivy visited his son he said, 'It's a hard world when you hit it, isn't it Bill!'

Accidents are usually a deterrent to speed-hungry young motorcyclists, but Bill took this in his stride. He learnt quickly, and his prang taught him to be wary of other road users; to be on his mettle the whole time in case anyone did something daft. But the incident did not slow him down; it just made him a wiser, more competent rider than before.

Bill loved to pit his skill against other motorcyclists, and he even enjoyed a few burn-ups with his doctor, who drove a Jaguar with considerable dash. But the insatiable desire for competition could not be fulfilled by the odd dice on public roads. Ivy yearned to race on the track with the feel of a pukka machine beneath him. Even so, he faced up to facts; it wasn't possible to purchase a competitive grass-tracker on a trainee mechanic's wages, so he resigned himself to the idea of waiting until he was a little older. Then, completely out of the blue, something turned up which changed everything.

Things were a bit slack at the shop one Wednesday, and Don Chisholm, who raced a KTT Velocette just for fun, decided to go up to Brands Hatch for a spin round. He asked Bill if he'd like to go along, too, and of course, the invitation was eagerly accepted.

At the time there was a 50cc Super Sports Itom in the shop, which had been taken in on a part-exchange deal. It was in road trim, but identical machines were being raced with pepped-up engines in the recently introduced 50cc class. This gave Don an idea, and he asked Bill if he would like a gallop round the track on the Itom. Needless to say Bill jumped at the chance, so the bike was checked over, loaded in the van, and they set off for the circuit.

Charlie Surridge was the only spectator at the track who took more than a casual interest in the tiny rider buzzing round on an equally tiny machine that afternoon. He'd done a bit of 50cc racing himself, so he clocked Bill on a few laps, and when he found that the lad was going very well he had a word with Don. Although Charlie was impressed, he probably had no idea that his remarks would provide a vital link in the making of a World Champion, but it was Charlie's words that set the Chisholm brothers thinking. Why didn't they convert the Itom and let Bill race it?

Needless to say, this suggestion met with great enthusiasm from Bill. The bike was suitably modified to make it competitive, and in a mid-season national event at Brands Hatch in 1959, W. D. Ivy, riding a 49cc Chis-Itom, lined up on the grid for his first road race. He rewarded his sponsors with a superb third place, behind Howard German and Roy Nicholson – two of the top 50cc riders in England.

The Chisholm team were very enthusiastic about that little bike, and most evenings they would all be working on it in an effort to squeeze a fraction more power out of the willing little engine. Their constant development of the bike did produce more speed, but at the expense of reliability, and Bill retired from several races with a seized engine until a separate oil feed to the crankshaft was devised, which solved the problem. At the following meeting at Brands, Bill led the whole field until the last lap. Then the oil feed pipe came off and he slowed. Realising what was wrong, he pushed it back with his hand and limped home second. Back in the paddock he was bitterly disappointed – fate had robbed him of his very first win.

Frank Sheene – Howard German's sponsor – congratulated the Chisholm team on a fine effort. Until then, nobody had provided a serious threat to the Sheene-Special on which German had established his superiority, and they were pleased that someone was at last giving them a run for their money.

'Never mind,' Frank told Bill, 'you set up a new lap record.' Hearing this news Bill really perked up again.

At the first meeting of the 1960 season, again at Brands, Bill romped away with the 50cc race, beating German in the process. In less than a season he had established himself among the top riders in the tiddler class, but Bill wanted to expand into the bigger classes as well, so he bought a 175cc Gilera road machine. He intended to convert it into racing trim, but the conversion was delayed, as was his racing for the remainder of that year, owing to a nasty road accident.

Whilst testing a Triumph, similar to his own, Bill crashed into a telegraph pole at speed, breaking both his legs and fracturing his pelvis. The Chisholm brothers had never seen a bike so totally wrecked; virtually everything was a write-off, even the engine and gearbox being shattered, such was the force of the impact.

When the brothers visited Bill in hospital they found him encased in plaster of Paris, propped up with pillows, with bits of balsa wood strewn all over the bed – helping some of the younger patients to make model aeroplanes! The cause of his prang, Bill explained, was that he had forgotten that the machine he was riding had lower footrests, unlike his own Triumph which he had modified for more ground clearance. From past experience he knew just how fast he could take the bend, so he went flying into it at his usual speed. The footrest dug into the road and off he came.

When Mrs Ivy went to see her son he told her, 'I didn't know there was so much pain in the world!'

Ivy was discharged from hospital a few weeks later with both legs in plaster. He hobbled round the house on crutches, bored stiff, until he discovered that he could work on motorcycles by laying on a blanket on the garage floor. By the time the plaster had been removed from one leg, Bill was driving his mother mad with his boredom. He wanted to return to work, so Mrs Ivy called in at the shop to see what could be done.

'Can you do *something* for him?' she asked the Chisholms. 'He's driving me mad, pestering the life out of me to come down here and see you. Is there anything you can give him to do to stop him from being so bored?'

The brothers said they would be glad to have Bill back, and they'd fix him up with something. So Mrs Ivy went back home and told the invalid that he could go back to work. 'But how will you get to and fro?' she asked, 'On the bus?'

'On the bus. . . .? No fear,' came the reply, '. . . on my motor-bike!'

In the mornings Mrs Ivy would wheel the Gilera out of the garage, help Bill on, strap the crutches to his back, and give him a good push to set him off down the hill. Once he got the engine going, Bill would give his mother a cheery wave and ride off to work. When he arrived at the shop he had to blow his horn to get someone to come out and help him off. In the evenings the system was reversed. Bill would be push-started outside Chisholm's – everyone used to turn out to see him off – and his mother would be waiting for him at home. Many people who encountered Bill on his journeys stopped to gaze in astonishment at the weird combination of crutches, plaster of Paris and small boy hurtling along on a motorcycle with gay abandon. He even drove his old Morris Eight car with his leg in plaster; unable to operate the clutch with his foot, he used a walking stick!

One evening, after Bill had stopped for a quick drink in a Maidstone pub (he only drank orange juice in those days), his old car refused to start. The battery was almost flat, and he was just about to go back into the pub for assistance when who should arrive but the local police. They noticed immediately that Bill was in difficulties, and young Ivy nearly had kittens when the two coppers came marching over to him. 'Is anything wrong?' they inquired, and when Bill explained why the car wouldn't start, they offered to give it a push. Neither noticed that the occupant's left leg was completely encased in plaster!

The policemen heaved and the car gathered momentum, with William perched at the controls, praying that the old beast would go. It coughed, spluttered, and eventually started, and the mightily relieved driver accelerated away, shouting his thanks out of the window, and leaving two very red-faced policemen panting in the road behind him. Once out of sight round the first corner, Bill exploded into laughter, and the incident so tickled his sense of humour on the journey home that it impaired his powers of navigation and upset the delicate application of his walking stick upon the clutch. If anyone in the vicinity of Maidstone had seen a Morris Eight that evening, being driven erratically by a young lad brandishing a walking stick and laughing uncontrollably, in all probability they would have assumed that the occupant was either a drunkard or an imbecile.

Even with one leg in plaster and the other in a very weak state, Bill still managed to get into his customary scrapes. A crowd of the boys couldn't get a grass-track bike started over at the farm, so Bill said, 'Let me have a go'. He handed his crutches to one of the boys, sat on the bike, and they pushed him down a steep country lane. He got the engine going halfway down the hill, stopped to turn round, lost his balance and fell over. Without crutches he could hardly stand, so he certainly couldn't get up with a motorcycle on top of him. The other lads started running to help, but before they reached Bill a car came round the corner and belted up the hill from the other direction! Fortunately, the driver saw the obstruction and slammed on his brakes in time, and a moment later the lads arrived on the scene, lifted the bike off Bill and helped him to his feet. When they handed him his crutches the car driver's eyes nearly popped out of his head!

Many people were convinced that Ivy's accident would put him off racing, but Bill was already planning his comeback.

'I'll be back on the track in time for the first meeting next season,' he announced with his usual confidence.

After spending over six months in plaster, and still far from fit, Bill Ivy stormed away with the 50cc race in the 1961 season-opener at Brands Hatch. And in the 250cc event he finished tenth on the Gilera, which had been increased to 190cc capacity by making a barrel out of old melted-down pistons and casting it in a biscuit tin.

Maurice Thomas also raced a '50' for the Maidstone team that year, and he and Bill figured prominently in the small-capacity races throughout the season. Then they teamed-up for the 50cc Enduro, held over 250 miles at Snetterton, in which each bike was to be shared by two riders. Despite losing 15 minutes replacing a broken throttle cable, the Chisholm team won, but four months later they were disqualified, although nobody really knew why. Apparently one of the other teams protested – Chisholm's never discovered who – the protest was upheld, and the second team declared the winners. The only thing that the Chisholm brothers could think of was that the disqualification was enforced because they refuelled once with the engine running.

Although the Gilera was a good machine on which to gain experience it was never really competitive. Even so, Ivy often finished among the first six, but he had reached the stage where he wanted something better. Race-kitted 125cc Honda road machines had just come on to the market, and as Chisholm's had an agency for the Japanese company they bought one. Bill finished well-up in his first race on the Honda, despite the fact that the bike was still completely standard; it even had silencers and lights on it. Afterwards, it was stripped, fitted with a race kit, and in Ivy's capable hands the Chis-Honda achieved consistently good placings.

At Brands, in the final meeting of the year, Bill was scrapping for the lead with Derek Minter and Rex Avery, who were riding the works EMCs – the fastest 125cc machines in the country at the time. Minter was the undisputed King of Brands and the English short circuits. Rounding Clearways in tight formation, Avery got into a slide and all three riders went down in a tangle at over 75 mph. Luckily, nobody was badly hurt, but both EMC riders received treatment for cuts and abrasions at the first-aid centre. Minter, his wounds attended to, got up to leave, while Avery was still being fussed over by several Red Cross girls. 'You want to watch him,' Derek said as he went out of the door. 'They don't call him "Sexy Rexy" for nothing!' Motorcycle racers are a crazy lot; even after throwing themselves down the road at speed, they still laugh and crack jokes.

Roy Francis, Bill's old school pal, had been working on the farm, but when his father decided to sell up he went to work with Bill. He had been helping at the shop in his spare time, and he always accompanied the team to race meetings when time permitted.

In those days, Chisholm's had two shops in Maidstone. Ivy was promoted to take charge of the smaller one, which dealt solely with repairs, and Roy was enlisted to help. They worked hard together and always did their best for their employers, but being high-spirited boys it was only natural that they should indulge in a certain amount of skylarking once away from the rather more sober atmosphere of the main shop. Roy has many happy memories of the laughs they had, and recalls a few incidents:

'We were fooling around one day and Bill started chasing me with a bucket full of water. I knew he wouldn't hesitate to throw it over me so I started dodging around, but finally he trapped me in a corner. Laughing triumphantly, he swung the bucket, but the bucket handle got hooked up on the handlebars of one of the bikes, emptying the water in the other direction – Bill got drenched from head to foot.

'Another time, he was being chased by one of the other mechanics. Seeking refuge in one of the outbuildings, Bill ran through an open doorway and slammed the door in his wake, without even glancing behind. The door was a glass one, and the other lad was running flat-out just a couple of paces behind. He just couldn't stop, and with a tremendous crash, ran straight through it, shattering it into a thousand pieces. Miraculously, he escaped injury without so much as a scratch. Chisholm's were told that a gust of wind had caught the door when it was open . . .

'Although I knew quite a bit about engines, Bill knew a lot more. If ever I was in trouble he would drop what he was doing to give me a hand, but one day the situation was reversed, and he came over to ask for my advice. He had completely stripped an engine and couldn't find anything wrong, although the customer had complained of a serious rattle. "I can't make it out," Bill said, "I've checked the whole engine and everything looks perfect." That was one problem I solved – he'd stripped the wrong bike down! We had two identical bikes in at the time, one due for a service, the other for an overhaul. Somehow, Bill had got them muddled-up!'

Racing was usually the main topic of conversation between the two lads, and they never tired of talking about riders, circuits and machines. Bill's attitude always impressed Roy, for although he admired top riders, he never held them in awe. 'They're only blokes on motorbikes,' Bill would say. 'They've only got two arms, two legs, and a head – same as me. If *they* can do it, *I* can do it!'

Roy had never given a thought to the idea of racing himself. He had just drifted into the role of Bill's mechanic. He enjoyed the atmosphere of the paddock, watching his pal ride, and he enjoyed helping out. Then one day Bill said, 'Why don't you have a go, Roy?'

The following Saturday was a general practice day at Brands. Bill loaned Roy his leathers and let him have a spin round on his Gilera. He went quite well, liked it, so decided to convert his road-going Honda and start competing. During the 1962 season both riders contested the same meetings and shared a transporter. Roy could never match Ivy's riding ability – the latter always threatened jokingly to lap him – but he steadily improved throughout the year.

1962 saw Ivy's Isle of Man début, in the 50cc TT, but luck was not with him and he retired on the first lap. However, on the short circuits his performances were rapidly improving and he was always up with the leaders on the Honda, and quite often won on the Itom.

At the tail-end of that season, Honda staged a marathon endurance test at Goodwood, with the idea of keeping three standard road machines running continuously for a whole week. Nineteen riders took part, taking shifts to keep the bikes going right round the clock. By the end of the week everyone was getting tired, and on the morning of the seventh day, Bill refused to get up for his stint until he'd had breakfast in bed. This was only an excuse for laying-in a little longer, but some of the boys took Bill at his word, lifted up his bed, loaded it into the back of a van, and drove to the near-by hotel that was catering for the whole team. On arrival, Bill and the bed were taken out and ceremoniously dumped on to the patio. Guests and staff looked on in surprised amusement and Bill's request was granted when a waiter came out and served him his breakfast. He was then loaded on to the van again and driven back to the circuit.

For 1963, Bill received an offer from Frank Sheene to race the 50cc Sheene-Special and a 125cc Bultaco, and after talking things over with the Chisholms, Ivy accepted. The brothers were 'a little bit sore' about losing their rider to their friendly rival, but they didn't want to stand in his way, for Frank's bikes were considerably more competitive. Roy took over the Chis-Honda, and of course Bill continued to work at the shop, even though he no longer raced for his employers.

The new partnership was an immediate success, so much so that Frank asked Bill whether he would like a trip to Spain to race at a meeting in Madrid. This suggestion met with great enthusiasm, but it also created a problem – time off work. Understandably, Chisholm's were not at all keen on giving Bill a week off when they were so busy, and they said they were sorry, but they just couldn't spare him. Bill could be extremely obstinate when he liked, especially when anything threatened to stand in the way of his racing; he got most upset, lost his temper in a big row with Don and Bill, and walked out. 'And I shan't be coming back, either,' Bill shouted, stomping out of the shop.

This incident occurred just a few days before the Spanish trip, and Bill had already told Frank that he would definitely go. In the heat of the moment, the little chap was dead serious when he told Chisholm's that he wasn't going to work for them any more, and straight after his row he went to the building site where Dave, his brother-in-law, worked, to see if he could get a job so that he could start working again on his return from Spain.

When Bill arrived at the building site there was a huge lorry load of bricks in, and the driver had just started unloading. He was a strapping great fellow, and made short work of shifting several thousand bricks by taking them off the lorry eight at a time. When he heard Bill asking for a job he burst out laughing. 'What *you*?' he said, 'A chap your size wouldn't last the morning out!'

Bill was still smouldering after his row with Chisholms, and this remark really sparked off his temper. Without a word, he jumped up on to the lorry and started taking the bricks off – eight at a time. Feeling a little humiliated, the lorry driver started working faster. Bill matched him, stack for stack. Everyone else stopped work to watch the silent trial of strength between the two on the lorry. With sweat pouring off them, they laboured side-by-side. The big fellow was nearly twice Ivy's size, and he worked flat-out in an effort to break him. Tiny he may have been, but Bill had an abundance of guts, and he never gave up. He was deceptively strong, especially in the arms, and could lift a five-gallon drum full of oil up to shoulder height at arm's length, but his legs were always weak after he broke them.

By the time the last brick had been unloaded both men were exhausted, but Bill had proved his point, and made the lorry driver look very small. There would be a job for Ivy when he came back from the Continent, if he still wanted it.

2

Ivy climbs up

FRANK SHEENE has never forgotten that journey to Madrid and back, which he recalls as a real adventure:

'Having only one entry at the meeting, in the 250cc class, I prepared a Yamaha for Bill, but due to last-minute preparations we were late setting off on the trip. We had only 26 hours to get from London to Madrid in time for the last practice session. Taking turns at the wheel of the transporter, we drove incessantly the whole way.

'Mid-way through the journey Bill decided to have a sleep. When he awoke he said, "You have a kip now, Frank, and I'll take over." Well, I never have been much of a one to sleep in a van when someone else is driving – somehow I always feel uneasy. It wasn't that Bill was a bad driver, but whenever anyone else drives I just can't seem to relax enough to go to sleep. However, we changed over, and as I felt very tired, I laid down in the back of the van. In a very short time I was almost asleep.

'We couldn't have travelled more than a few miles, when all of a sudden there was an almighty bang. The van lurched and I was flung across the floor. Petrified, I sat up and shouted, "What's the matter, Bill? . . . What's happened?"

'"Oh, it's all right, we've only run up the bank – don't worry." Bill replied.

'He hadn't really woken-up properly when he took over, and in a half-dozy state he'd drifted across the road, on to the grass verge and up the bank. That incident woke both of us up, and I didn't get a wink of sleep afterwards.

'In spite of getting two punctures during the journey, we finally arrived at the circuit, just in time for the final practice sessions. Most of the others had been practising the day before as well, and the quick riders were going pretty rapidly by this time. We hurriedly unloaded the bike, Bill changed into his leathers, and I said, "I don't know what the gearing will be like, but we haven't got time to change it now, so you'd better get out there, Bill."

'So out he went, and in no time at all he was flying round. Then he got mixed up in a bit of a skirmish with two Spanish riders, and to my surprise, he was soon lapping within a couple of seconds of the fastest practice times. The amazing thing was he'd never seen the track before in his life!

'Well, he came back in and said, "I think I can knock a bit more off that, Frank." So off he went on his second attempt, and Bill being Bill he did try to clip a bit more off and came to grief. It wasn't really his fault because two Spanish riders wouldn't give way to him. If they had, Bill would probably have been OK, but they didn't, and off he came. The trouble was, the other riders were local chaps, and they didn't take too kindly to an unknown foreigner blowing them off on their home circuit. By the time I got to the spot where it happened Bill had disappeared, so I collected the bike and wheeled it back to the pits. I hadn't a clue where he'd gone, and not speaking any Spanish, I had rather a job trying to find out where he was. Eventually I found out that he'd been driven away in the ambulance.

'After the practice finished I learnt (with some difficulty) from the officials that Bill had been taken to hospital. This was ten o'clock in the morning, so I started looking for the hospital, but at half-past-six that night I *still* hadn't found the right one! Eventually I ran into this chap who spoke a little English. I asked him if he knew where Bill might have been taken, and he said, "Yes – *I am the ambulance driver!* I know where Ivy is."

'Apparently he'd been looking all over the place for me as I'd been looking all over the place for Bill. . . . Anyway, he took me round the back streets to this tiny little building – it was a beautiful little place, but it wasn't a hospital, it was an ambulance station – and there, sitting on the stone floor with about five nurses round him, was Bill. "Where the hell have you been?" he asked. He'd been waiting all day for me and had become more than a little concerned when I had failed to turn up by lunchtime. He hadn't a clue where to go; he couldn't speak a word of Spanish; we hadn't had time to book in a hotel, so he didn't have a place to go to; and he wondered what on earth was the matter because I hadn't turned up. Fortunately, he was only slightly injured, so off we went to find some lodgings.

'We soon found somewhere to stay, and by this time both of us were dog-tired, so we parked the van outside the hotel, went up to our rooms and laid down. We hadn't been upstairs for more than five minutes when there was a loud banging on the front door. It was the police. They told us that we had to move the van as it was parked in the wrong place, so after a lot of grumbling and muttering unprintable things about Spanish policemen, Bill went outside and shifted the van about 50 yards down the road. But we hadn't been upstairs for more than 10 minutes when there was another banging session on the front door. It was the police again! They insisted that we should again move the van as it was still in a restricted area. By this time, Bill was very angry. "I'm *not* going to move it. Why couldn't they tell us where they wanted it parked in the first place, instead of just telling us to shift it?" he said. Eventually, I persuaded him to come down. I said, "Look, Bill, if we don't do as they say they'll put us inside." So down we went again and clambered back in the van. The policeman was babbling away and waving his arms about trying to give directions, but Bill, sitting in the driver's seat, hadn't a clue what he was trying to say, and was getting most annoyed with the whole business, so he leant out of the window and shouted, "Oi – *get stuffed!*" The policeman, obviously ignorant of the message, replied, "Si, si, yes – just over there," and gesticulated fiercely to emphasise the exact spot where he wanted the van parked. After placing the van precisely where instructed we went back to the hotel, and thankfully the rest of the day passed off without further incident.

'The following morning we straightened-out the bike (the damage was only superficial) and went to the circuit. But Bill's fall had aggravated his old leg injury and he could hardly walk, so push-starting was obviously out of the question. I asked the organisers if they would allow Bill to be started by a pusher, and they agreed, provided that he started from the rear of the grid. When the riders started forming up ready for the off, Bill sat on the bike, with me standing alongside ready to give him a good push when the flag dropped, then the officials began clearing the starting area, hustling mechanics and everyone away from the grid. "All off, all off," they shouted. I tried to explain that I had permission to push-start my rider as he was injured, but they didn't understand, and the officials were furious because I wouldn't budge. They shouted at me, pushed me, and when that didn't do any good they called over two policemen who escorted me off the track. Bill was left on his own, right at the rear of the line-up with nobody to help him start.

'The flag dropped and Bill pushed, but he was hobbling so badly that he could hardly move the thing at all. After struggling for about 60 yards he was exhausted, then finally the engine fired, and away he went. The rest of the field by then were coming round the back of the circuit – we were nearly a lap behind.

'Bill rode like a demon. He chased after them, he caught them, he passed most of them, and he was lying *second* when the gear linkage came adrift. He had no alternative but to retire. The footrest had been bent in his practice spill, and when I straightened it, it must have weakened because it just snapped. And as the gear linkage was attached to the footrest it came off with it. It was very disappointing for both of us, for Bill had ridden a fantastic race. The Spaniards were very impressed, and Señor Bulto, head of the Bultaco motorcycle company, said, "Who is this man Ivy? You seem to have an aptitude for picking good riders, and this one is outstandingly good."'

On his return from Spain, Bill swallowed his pride and went to see Chisholm's, the quarrel was patched-up, and he continued to work at the shop. He rode Frank Sheene's bikes throughout the year with considerable success, and in the 50cc TT he finished a creditable seventh, but in the 125cc event the Bultaco spluttered to a halt on the first lap when the carburettor needle-clip broke.

Towards the end of the year Geoff Monty, the Twickenham motorcycle dealer, supplied Ivy with a Yamaha and a Norton. Geoff had first met Bill at the Goodwood marathon the previous season, and it had not escaped his eye that Ivy had pushed the little Hondas round quicker than the other riders. During the event, Bill had asked Geoff if he would give him a try-out on a big bike, and Monty had said he would think about it. 'I was impressed by his enthusiasm as well as his obvious riding ability,' Geoff recalls, 'and he was very persistent. After asking me again, I gave him a Norton for the August meeting at Brands Hatch.'

This meeting proved to be Ivy's best during 1963, for he caused a sensation in the 125cc race by battling with Tommy Robb on a saturated track. Robb was mounted on a semi-works Honda, a far superior machine to the Sheene-Bultaco. The pair fought it out for the entire race, and with a splendid display of fast riding on a treacherous surface, Ivy only lost a victory by half a wheel. Proving that this was no fluke, he again finished second to Robb in the 250cc event on a Yamaha.

Unable to obtain an entry on Monty's 350cc Norton in the 350cc class, Bill entered the 500cc and unlimited races, and despite the speed disadvantage he finished in seventh and fifth places, respectively, amongst some of the best big-bike riders in the country. It was in these races that Ivy gave a first glimpse of his amazing versatility, for it was his first race on a big machine, apart from a solitary outing on Chisholms' old Velocette. Monty was very impressed, and he decided to sponsor Bill for the remainder of the season.

The Chisholm brothers were keen to have Bill riding for them again in 1964, but they realised that they would have to provide him with a competitive machine. It was obvious that Ivy was going to be better than just another good rider, so it wasn't fair to hamper his progress by giving him anything that wasn't capable of winning. The obvious choice for the 125cc class was a CR93 Honda production racer. These superbly engineered little bikes were very similar to the twin-cylinder works machines; only just introduced on to the market, they were the best that money could buy in their class. Chisholms' put their proposal to Bill, he accepted, and an order was placed for one of the Hondas there and then to ensure that it arrived well in time for the start of the following season. It was at this moment that Ivy formed his first racing ambition. 'I want to try to win a British Championship next year,' he told his parents.

Geoff Monty agreed to supply machines for all solo classes except the 125, and Bill decided to drop the 50cc class altogether. With two sponsors and four bikes at his disposal, Ivy's prospects looked good.

One rather amusing incident occurred after Bill's first ride for Monty. The Norton had been loaned on the basis that Bill should transport it to the meeting himself, and return it a few days afterwards. But when he turned up with the bike still covered in track grime, Geoff promptly told him to take it back home and clean it. This was done, and Bill returned with the Norton really gleaming; it was some years later when Geoff discovered that Roy Francis had been responsible for cleaning it! That was one chore which Bill hated.

Another incident, which occurred at Chisholms', had everyone in stitches. An elderly lady brought her moped along for attention, and Bill repaired the machine, and when she collected it he wheeled it outside for her. She thanked him, and then, assuming that he was only a young lad, said, 'And I suppose *you'll* have a motorbike when you grow up?' With a supreme effort, Bill managed to keep a straight face, and replied, 'Yes, I will!'

When the new CR93 Honda arrived at the shop, Bill and Roy couldn't unwrap it fast enough. 'I *must* have a ride on it,' Bill said. So he started it up and rode it round the block a couple of times. The high-pitched scream of the tiny exhausts was terrific as Ivy sped round the back streets of Maidstone, and the wail continued for several minutes, echoing around the surrounding buildings in sharp contrast to the drone of traffic on the busy roads near by. Inevitably, the commotion attracted the unwanted attention of the Law, who arrived on the scene a few moments after Ivy had completed his 'laps' and returned the bike to the workshop. Unable to discover the source of the noise, the policemen became suspicious and went into the shop in search of a few clues. 'Yes,' Bill told them 'there was a young tearaway riding round on a motorbike without silencers – but he seems to have gone now!'

In his first race on the Honda, Bill finished second at Mallory Park, and the following weekend, on a wet track at Brands Hatch, he led the 125cc race from the drop of the flag. Then, on the second lap, the slippery surface at Druids Hill Bend caught him out, and Ivy and Honda parted company in spectacular fashion. Most riders would have given up, but not Bill. From a seemingly hopeless last position he tore through the field and caught up to eighth place by the finish. Tommy Robb won the race, and afterwards he said to Ivy, 'What on earth did you do that for? You had the beating of all of us at the speed you were going – then you went a bit faster and fell off!'

Further meetings at Mallory and Brands produced good results for Ivy. In the 125cc events he won at Mallory in record speed, but at Brands it was Chris Vincent who pushed him into an unwelcome second spot. In the 250cc events Bill was also performing very consistently, usually finishing between third and fifth places. On the bigger bikes it was largely a matter of gaining experience and learning how to cope with a heavier, more powerful mount. However, Ivy was doing very well, and at Brands he raised a few eyebrows by leading Derek Minter in an unlimited race before running out of petrol. Derek had helped Bill quite a lot, and they were good friends, but Bill held a burning ambition to beat his idol. He hoped that one day he would be good enough to de-throne the 'King' on his home track.

It wasn't too long before part of that ambition was achieved, for Ivy beat Minter in a 250cc race at Snetterton. *Motor Cycle News* covered the meeting, and here is an extract from their race report:

'In the 250cc race Derek Minter was dicing with Bill Ivy for second place. On laps two and three Derek was in command, then Bill took over. But on the final lap, as they approached the line, it was Derek ahead once more. Bill's superb timing, however, which has shown itself on numerous occasions this year, stood him in good stead, and a matter of yards from the finish he pulled out of Minter's slipstream and got the verdict.'

For the first part of the season Chris Vincent was usually the top man in the 125cc races, much to Bill's frustration. Although he was usually second, only a short way behind, Ivy simply was not content, and he resolved that the only way to beat Vincent was to go faster. 'If one person can do it, then so should another,' Bill told himself – and he did just that. From that moment on, the combination of Ivy and Chis-Honda were virtually unbeatable. Race and lap records tumbled everywhere in a phenomenal run of success. If Ivy was down to race his Honda in the programme, then that race was virtually a foregone conclusion. Only when the ultra-fast works machines put in an occasional appearance on the short circuits was the outcome ever in doubt. Even then, Ivy would be snapping at their heels, cornering magnificently to offset what he lost down the straights. Usually, he had to give best in the end, to sheer speed alone, but he never gave up trying. On two occasions he actually beat the works men at Brands Hatch.

Only one person stood between Bill and the 125cc British Championship, which, at that time, was known as the AC-U Star. The title, decided on a points system, lay between Dave Simmonds, who rode an ex-works Japanese Kawasaki, and Ivy. Simmonds had amassed the bulk of his points early in the season, beating both Vincent and Ivy at two meetings, and he led the title chase at the halfway stage.

Realising that he needed as many points as he could get, and that he had not entered the Castle Combe meeting where eight valuable points could be picked up for a win, Bill took over Roy Francis' entry and scored a runaway victory. He also raised the lap record by over 3 mph on his first visit to the Wiltshire circuit.

Ivy didn't grow much, but his reputation did. Although his successes were achieved mainly in the lightweight classes, on the Honda and Geoff Monty's 250cc Cotton, it was his performances on the bigger machines which endeared him to a growing army of fans. Spectators delighted in the spectacle of Ivy snaking his way through a bend on the 650 Triumph-engined Monard, and they

c

marvelled at the skill of such a tiny rider who appeared almost dwarf-like in comparison to the huge machine beneath him. The Monard was a special, the brainchild of Geoff Monty, and there was a 500cc version as well. Both were competitive enough to enable Bill to finish consistently in the first six, but because of his light weight he often found them a handful on bumpy corners.

Monty managed to fix Bill up with a ride on a 250cc ex-works Yamaha at Brands Hatch, and Bill won the race by a mile and enthused afterwards, 'It's the most exciting bike I've ever ridden – I wouldn't like to say which is quicker, the Yamaha or Geoff's 650! At the start of the race it was only running on one cylinder, then it suddenly chimed in on two. I've never known anything like it, because the front wheel leapt in the air, and all I had to do to win was hang on.'

One asset Ivy had, and one which was to prove invaluable later in his career, was an aptitude for learning circuits remarkably quickly. On his very first outing at Cadwell Park he won the 125 race, breaking the lap record; was second in the 250 after an atrocious start, and established another lap record; then he forced his way to another second place in the big race after being left on the grid.

Another amazing thing was his consistency. In Geoff Monty's opinion Ivy could never ride badly. 'He just couldn't,' said Geoff, 'he had so much natural ability. I don't know of any rider I've had anything to do with – ever – who had as much natural ability as he did. What Bill lacked in height and weight, (not strength, because he was immensely strong, as strong as anyone) was more than offset by his tremendous amount of nerve and determination. He just *had* to win races if he could.'

So the season wore on, and Bill, always having yearned for a big, fast car, found that his financial resources would almost stretch to the purchase of a nice 3.4 Jaguar he'd seen up for sale at a local garage. Almost, but not quite, until some of Bill's friends clubbed together and loaned him a bit more cash. The Jaguar was duly bought, and it was agreed that all the boys would use the car when they went out in the evenings, and they all clubbed together to buy petrol, which the car simply drank. These outings were a great success, for chatting up the 'dollies' (as Bill always called them) was no trouble at all when you had a Jag. They dashed all over the place, 'terrorising' the girls from Maidstone to Hastings, and the car was affectionately christened 'the crumpet wagon'.

Bill was really chuffed with his new car, and he loved to speed along trying to blow everyone else off the road, but he soon found that he couldn't throw the Jaguar round a corner with the same gay abandon as he could a motorcycle, and he had more than one hair-raising incident before he began to master the technique of handling four wheels with any degree of finesse.

Dave and Sue were out driving one Sunday afternoon when they met Bill coming down a very steep hill from the opposite direction. He was completely out of control and the car was spinning round and round in circles, with Bill fighting at the wheel in a desperate attempt to get the thing pointing in the right direction again. Although he spun almost the whole way down the hill – just missing Sue and Dave on the way – Bill finally managed to get everything under control by the time he got to the bottom, and he didn't hit a thing. The next time Dave saw his little brother-in-law, he said, 'Did you enjoy yourself coming down Dover Hill the other day?' But Bill only laughed as though it had been nothing.

Such incidents would deter the average driver from going quickly for months, perhaps for good, but to Ivy mastering anything on wheels at speed was a challenge. He accepted the danger as part of it; it was the penalty for making a mistake, and no amount of frightening occurrences would stop him from trying to go faster, but he always learnt from his mistakes.

Another time he got into a skid, left the road, and headed for some trees at a most alarming rate. 'Thought me end had come, Ethel. I didn't think I could possibly avoid every tree, but I tried weaving in and out of them and somehow I got through,' Bill told his mother afterwards. Mrs Ivy would scold him, telling him that it was silly trying to go so fast, but he would only laugh.

A great one for nicknames, Bill always called his mother 'Ethel', and because he was a fan of the Beatles, Mr Ivy had the distinction of being dubbed 'Ringo'. Roy Francis was known as 'The General', a nickname which Bill had instigated during their schooldays. It derived from Francis, to 'Franco', to 'General Franco' (after the Spanish dictator), and finally the 'Franco' was dropped. The name had stuck at school, but afterwards everybody used Roy's real name except Bill, who insisted on using the term 'General' wherever they were and in whatever the company, much to the embarrassment of his friend. 'I used to cringe when Bill used my nickname in front of a crowd,' said Roy, 'and when people would say, "*What* did he call you?" I used to say, "I don't know".' To his friends, Bill was known as 'Willie', or 'Wee Willie'.

Roy and Bill were still great friends, and the former continued to help at race meetings despite having to attend to his own machine.

Although slightly envious, Roy was never jealous of his pal's success, in fact he was very proud of him, and even though Bill was fast becoming a star his attitude was no different from before; he was still the same old Bill, and hadn't changed a scrap.

After normal working hours at the shop the boys would sometimes work in the evenings, preparing their machines for the next meeting, and it was quite late one night when they decided to pack up. Bill chose to use an 83cc MV for going home, instead of taking the car, and as Roy was using his road bike, they set off together with Bill leading on the little MV. They had gone some way when Roy noticed a light behind him. Glancing round, he saw a motorcycle catching them up. 'Coppers', thought Roy, and immediately flashed his lights at Bill to warn him, then slowed down because they were approaching a 30 mph limit. It *was* a policeman, and realising that there was a likely 'catch' in front, he overtook Roy and sat on Bill's tail. The latter, thinking that his pal was trying to overtake him, shot round a series of bends in typical racing style, then had the shock of his life on the next straight when the stern-faced policeman roared past on the big Triumph and waved him down. That incident cost Bill £7 and an endorsement.

Apart from testing machines at the shop, Ivy didn't ride on the roads very often. One day when he was out on a test he ran into Mr Cocksedge, his old schoolmaster. 'I had a scooter in those days,' recalls Mr Cocksedge, 'and as I pulled up at some traffic lights I heard a "thump, thump" behind me, and this massive great motorbike pulled up alongside with Bill on it. He kept revving up and nearly blowing me off my saddle. "Whato," he said. "Whato," I replied, and we grinned at each other. Then the lights changed and this huge bike, with what looked like a small boy on it, just went "whoosh" . . . and he shot off leaving me in a cloud of smoke.

'Whenever I had trouble with the scooter I always took it to Chisholms', and Bill would see to it personally for me. He would say, "Oh, I'll sort it out and pop it round to the school for you this afternoon." And when he delivered it, he used to take a great delight in coming round the bends by the playground leaning right over. In fact I've never seen a scooter go over at such an angle and still adhere to the road.'

At race meetings, Ivy was not only gaining in popularity with the fans, but also with the other riders and officials. There was always considerable hilarity in the paddocks when he was around. He was a fun-loving young man, with a happy-go-lucky manner, but once on the track he was a serious and very formidable opponent. Only once, at Snetterton, did his skylarking interfere with his racing. Geoff got one of the bikes ready for the next race, but Bill was nowhere to be seen. After the race had started Bill came dashing up, 'Was I supposed to be out for that one?' he asked. Geoff said that he was. 'Oh dear', said Bill. He had been having a laugh and a joke with some of the lads in the far corner of the paddock and had forgotten all about the racing until he heard the roar of the pack starting, but he never, ever missed a race again.

In two British championship rounds, one at Snetterton and the other at Brands, Ivy scored two vital 125cc victories. In the former he beat his closest challenger, Dave Simmonds, and at Brands he maintained a four-second lead over Chris Vincent for almost the entire race. Vincent was really trying, but he could make no impression on the leader, although he never lost ground. Ivy was well on the way to his first championship win.

When Bill turned up at the Race of the Year meeting at Mallory Park he opened the boot of his Jaguar, and out jumped two girls, much to everyone's astonishment. The girls had been hitch-hiking to the track, so Bill picked them up, invited them into the paddock, then realised that he hadn't any spare passes. So he stopped a little way before the circuit, persuaded the girls to get into the boot and smuggled them in. The incident was even more amusing when it was learnt that Mike Hailwood had given his passes to his mechanics, and the gatekeeper refused to let him in until he paid £1. However, it was a good investment, for Mike won the big race and the £1,000 that went with it; Bill finished sixth.

At the season's curtain call at Brands Hatch, Ivy rounded-off a magnificent year with some fine riding. He set his seal on the 125 title by winning yet again, and as the best eight performances of each rider counted, he scored maximum points with eight wins. Vincent was in a very determined mood that day, and he led during the early stages of the race, and it was obvious that he was out to avenge his earlier defeats at Ivy's hands. But unfortunately he tried too hard, and round Westfield Bend Vincent and the Honda went their separate ways, almost fetching Bill down with them. From then on Ivy won as he pleased, whilst his rival was taken to the first-aid centre with a lacerated face. Vincent, an extremely versatile performer on both solo and sidecars, refused to go to hospital until he had contested the sidecar race, which he won in his usual style despite being bandaged like an Egyptian mummy. Afterwards, he dashed off to get the wound stitched up.

Although Derek Minter was still the acknowledged King of

Brands, Ivy had earned the title of Crown Prince. He followed his 125cc win with a second place, in front of Minter, in the 250 event, and gained leaderboard positions in the big races. But during the meeting Tom Kirby, one of the top private motorcycle sponsors in Europe, told Bill, 'At present Minter is the King and you're the Crown Prince. You'll be the King one day, but you're not going to make it if you keep racing like you do.'

'Racing like I do? What do you mean, Uncle?' All the riders called Tom 'Uncle'.

'You're riding in nearly every solo race, and in an afternoon that's anything up to *seven* races. It's too much for a little fella like you!', advised Tom.

Bill was most indignant. 'To hell with me size,' he said, '*I'm not tired!*'

Tom explained that although he might not *feel* tired, this was because he was young. 'But if you keep it up, it might have an effect on your riding later on. What you want to do is to restrict yourself to the main classes, the 350 and 500's,' said Tom.

To which Bill replied, 'OK then, if I'm going to do that I'll ride your bikes!' He had always hoped that Tom would ask him to race a pair of his immaculate machines, but 'Uncle' only smiled at this remark. He thought Bill was joking.

With the racing over until March 1965 the Winter was a time for relaxing and socialising. It came as a welcome break after the hectic schedule of a long season, and the 'dollie-chasing' outings in the Jaguar and the parties helped to pass the time quite pleasantly.

A whole crowd of them went down to Hastings for a party one weekend. One was a big chap, not tall, but very broad and strong, and during the evening, some fellow who was a total stranger started to make a nuisance of himself. He was well intoxicated, so everybody decided that he should go. Bill and his big friend escorted him to the door, but he started cutting up rough and took a swing with his fist, so Bill stepped in and hit him. Apparently it was like something out of a silent movie, for the force of Bill's punch knocked the fellow over backwards, and he landed in an empty pram which sailed off down the hallway. Furthermore, he was completely unconscious!

When he came round the first thing he said, addressing Bill's friend was, 'What did you do that for?' When told, 'It wasn't me – it was Bill,' he was convinced his leg was being pulled; he just couldn't believe that anyone so small could pack such a wallop.

However, Bill's action had the desired effect. The stranger was no longer quarrelsome, in fact he was very subdued, and they all left the party on the best of terms.

Reflecting on his rider's performances over the 1964 season, Geoff Monty was very impressed, and he considered that every race had been outstanding. That year, Bill had been under contract to him, but for 1965 Monty decided that to tie Ivy to a contract might jeopardise his chances of getting a works ride, and it was obvious that he was going to be that good. As Monty didn't want to stand in Bill's way if an opportunity arose, it was agreed to continue their arrangement on a gentleman's agreement, and if Ivy was offered better machines he would be free to take them .

The Chisholm brothers were delighted with the championship win, and Bill, despite Uncle Tom's advice, decided to continue riding the little Honda. After all, he had a title to defend. Unlike his set-up with Monty (who did all the work and transported the bikes to the meetings), Bill prepared the Chis-Honda himself and transported the bike on a trailer hitched to his car.

From the drop of the flag at the Mallory Park season-opener in 1965, Ivy was in stupendous form. In the three races he finished, his lowest placing was fourth. It was the same at Brands Hatch a fortnight later, and again at Snetterton the following week. Then came the Easter weekend, which began with the Good Friday meeting at Brands. Bill even entered the 50cc race, which he won. He was second behind Hugh Anderson's works Suzuki in the 125 event, and in chasing Anderson he established a new lap record. Only Mike Duff, on another works machine – a Yamaha – was better than Bill in the 250 race; and to cap it all the Crown Prince chased the King all the way in the 500 battle to finish second.

This was the pattern all the way over Easter, in a hectic, muscle-aching schedule which involved driving from Kent to Snetterton in Norfolk, on to Oulton Park in Cheshire, then finally down to Mallory Park in Leicestershire. In all, Ivy rode in over 20 races, and even he had to admit that he felt 'a little bit weary' afterwards. Riders and spectators alike marvelled at him – they couldn't understand where he got the energy from.

At the final meeting of the Easter series Bill romped away with both lightweight races, but in the 350 event he fell at the hairpin, hurting his arm. Towards the end of the day, Geoff Monty thought that his rider was acting a little strangely, but when Bill told him that he didn't want to race the big bikes any more he was astounded.

He just couldn't understand it, for he knew that Bill was the last person to be put off by a spill.

'Look,' Geoff said, 'you've knocked yourself about a bit today, Bill, and you've had a hard weekend. You don't want to make rash decisions now. Go home, get a good night's rest, and see how you feel tomorrow. Then give me a ring tomorrow evening.' Bill agreed to this, and they set off home, with Geoff pondering on what Bill had said; he was puzzled, for the little chap didn't seem to be himself at all.

Bill phoned his sponsor the next evening as arranged, and after learning that the injured arm was all right, apart from being 'a bit stiff', Geoff asked Bill if he had made up his mind about what he was going to do. There was an uneasy silence, then came a stammered reply which shook him rigid. 'I'm sorry,' Bill said, 'but I won't be able to ride your bikes any more . . . *I'm going to ride for Tom Kirby!*'

3

Uncle Tom Kirby

GEOFF WAS ANGRY and rather bitter about the whole business. It wasn't that Bill had left him without warning that annoyed him as much as the excuse he had made about not wanting to ride the big bikes any more. Prior to Easter, the 'grapevine' had buzzed with rumours of Ivy practising on Kirby's machines at Brands Hatch, but Geoff hadn't believed them at the time. Only when Bill revealed that he was leaving to join Kirby's team did he realise that they must have been true.

The motorcycling press were sympathetic towards Monty. The general opinion was that it wasn't fair for a rider suddenly to leave his sponsor without notice mid-way through the season. *Motor Cycle* carried the headlines 'SHOCK FOR MONTY – IVY JOINS KIRBY', and part of the report read:

'Twickenham sponsor Geoff Monty had a nasty shock last week. For, only a day after a highly successful weekend, his rider Bill Ivy rang Geoff to say that he wouldn't be riding for him anymore. He'd decided to race Tom Kirby's machines. This means that bang in the middle of the busiest racing time of the year, Geoff is left without a pilot for his very successful machines. Naturally, he's not exactly delighted: "I think I might have been given a bit of warning. The first I knew was when Bill rang me," he said ruefully.'

Bill was quoted as saying: 'I don't like upsetting anyone, but I want to race an AJS and a Matchless, and I want to do the TT.' Monty admitted that he could not afford to supply Ivy with three machines for the costly Isle of Man races.

So Bill was slightly out of favour at the time, and even some of his fans didn't think much of his actions. In the public eye Ivy emerged from the situation with his image a fraction tarnished, but everyone soon forgot the incident in the devastating run of success which followed the new Ivy–Kirby partnership. However, the reason for Bill's switch, and the behind-the-scenes story of why he changed camps was never unfurled publicly. Consequently, very few people knew the facts.

In fact, Bill had approached Kirby for a ride before the season started, but Tom had turned him down because he didn't like the idea of taking on a rider who was already sponsored. 'Sponsors are hard to find,' he had told Bill, 'and when you get a good one you should stick to him. I don't want to come between you and Geoff Monty.'

Ivy was not ungrateful for Monty's efforts, but he realised that the big Monards, although competitive, were not quite good enough consistently to challenge the top men. Up against the Nortons of John Cooper or Derek Minter, or the Kirby-Matchless ridden by South African Paddy Driver, the Monard was at a slight disadvantage; you couldn't give anything away to riders of that calibre and expect to beat them. A less ambitious rider possibly would have been content, but Bill Ivy was not content to finish behind such men. To him, even second place was second best. He knew that he stood a fair chance of beating his rivals if he had machines equal to theirs, or something a little lighter which he could throw around easier than the Monard. The superbly prepared Kirby bikes fitted the bill on both counts, and they appealed to Ivy more than anything short of a works thoroughbred.

More than anything, Ivy wanted to become a full-time professional, and he knew that he had to do just that bit better in order to survive financially. He certainly couldn't pack up his job and race for a living on Monty's bikes, for Geoff had to take a 50 per cent cut of all the winnings and appearance money to help towards the cost of running the machines. On the other hand Kirby's runners pocketed all their appearance and prize money, for the team received financial backing from the Shell/BP oil company, which subsidised the high costs of running the team. Bill knew that if he rode for Uncle Tom he stood an excellent chance of achieving his ambition.

Shortly after the season started Ivy approached Kirby again, and this time they had a long discussion about it. Although Tom was keen to have Bill riding for him, he still didn't like the idea of 'stealing' a rider from another sponsor. It was only when Bill said that he was going to leave Monty anyway, even if Tom didn't want him, that Kirby finally changed his mind. He knew that the Maidstone lad was right in that he needed the right machines if he was ever to get right to the top and turn professional, so he agreed to give Ivy a try-out:

'We went down to Brands on the Wednesday before Easter. Mike Hailwood came along, too, because I'd promised him bikes for the short-circuit meetings when his works MV wasn't available, and he wanted to test them. There was nothing better for me, seeing Mike and Bill out on the track together on two of my 500cc G50s, having a real go. The pair of them just went round faster and faster. In the end they were lapping within a fraction of the lap record, and thoroughly enjoying themselves.

'Afterwards, Mike said, "Tom, you can't do anything but give him his chance – he's proved it to me. He's now showing that, in spite of his size, with a good 500 he can do battle. When I was out there I was really trying on your bike, and I couldn't shake him off!" That certainly convinced me that Bill was the boy for the future. He surprised me and everyone else (including himself) by just how quickly he went; he took to those bikes like a duck to water. So I said, "Right. If your mind is made up, Bill, and you're definitely set on leaving Geoff Monty, I will offer you the machines".'

Ivy was elated, but one thing worried him – the nagging thought of how he was going to break the news to Monty. He tried to put it out of his mind until the last meeting of the Easter weekend, and resolved to do his very best in his final races for Monty. Then, when the time came, he started to make a clean breast of it but somehow his courage failed him, and he ended up inventing the excuse about not wanting to race the bigger machines any more because he'd fallen off. It was the classic case of an inexperienced young man in an awkward situation, and not quite knowing how to handle it. On the one hand, ambition was driving him on; and on the other, there was the feeling of guilt in letting Monty down. However, if one is to succeed, sentiment must not be allowed to stand in the way of opportunities, and without being ruthless or unkind there comes a time in everyone's life when it is best to move on. Geoff Monty had provided a vital stepping-stone in Ivy's career, but he was limited in what he could do. As a one-man effort he had done as well as anyone could do in his position, but the Kirby team had so much more to offer. It was a much larger concern with a large stable of competitive machinery, a commercial organisation run along works-team lines, and recognised as being the best privately entered team in the world. Only a place in a

factory team was considered better. Monty expected that some-
time during the season he would lose his rider, but thought it
would be to a factory team; he certainly hadn't anticipated that
Ivy would go to another private sponsor. But although he had
hoisted Bill up another rung in the ladder of success, Geoff had had
his reward with some magnificent performances, so really the score
was even.

Despite adverse comments in the Press, Kirby decided that he
would not publicly defend Ivy's action in leaving Monty to join
him.

'I was not going to make anything of it – we said nothing. It was
up to Bill to go out on to the track and prove that he had made the
right decision, and to prove that my choice in him was right – and
he went out and proved it. He'd already set his sights on beating
Minter, and he did just that in his first ride on the G50 Matchless
by winning the 500cc race at Brands Hatch.'

After his highly successful début Ivy went to Snetterton the
following weekend, and staved-off desperate attempts by John
Cooper and Derek Minter to win the 500cc final. It was the same at
Mallory Park. Bill won three of the four solo events and set up a new
race record in his victorious ride on the big Kirby-Matchless. The
motorcycling Press headlines told virtually the same story every
week: 'BILL IVY'S GOLDEN LAPS' – 'BILL IVY LICKS
THEM ALL' – '3 WINS AND A RECORD – BILL IVY'S
BEST YET" – and so it went on.

One or two of the star riders resented being beaten, but they
licked their wounds and resolved to do better. They weren't going
to be de-throned without a fight, and they tried everything to oust
Ivy from the front. As a result, the races became even more hectic,
and the battles more intense, until sometimes it was frightening to
watch. Ivy had to have his wits about him, for he had become the
target, the man they were all trying to beat; the positions had been
reversed and the hunter was now the hunted. For the crowds, the
struggles for supremacy were awe-inspiring and thrilling spectacles, but in the middle of the fighting, jostling pack at the head of
the field, it was no place for the faint-hearted.

Cornering at speeds of up to 90 mph, toes scraping the tarmac.
Flashing down the straights, head under the windscreen. Slipstreaming a rival, a mere foot away from his rear wheel at over
120 mph. Sometimes weaving down the straight, trying to stop a
rival from slipstreaming and getting a 'tow'. Hurtling towards

bends, each man determined to brake last in a desperate attempt to draw away from the pack. Diving into bends, inches apart, occasionally rubbing shoulders. Powering out, with rear wheels kicking and sliding over the bumps. Changing up through the gears again and away down the next straight, exhausts bellowing defiantly. Challenging – being challenged; overtaking – being overtaken; out-braking – being out-braked; leaning on – being leant on . . . the cut-and-thrust, exacting, terrifying, exhilarating world of road racing. A world apart, fraught with danger and excitement, experienced by few, yet watched by many.

For Bill Ivy, this was the supreme test. More than once, riders who found they could not beat him by out-riding him, tried to frighten him into submission, but he lacked nothing in guts and was quick to give as he got in the way of hard-riding tactics. He experienced all this in challenging the cream of Britain's short-circuit aces. He took the best they could give, and he emerged victorious.

Uncle Tom was delighted, but he worried like hell when Bill first rode for him because he knew that the little chap was having a tough time. He admired the way in which his rider would not be intimidated into accepting defeat, but he was very angry when Bill came in from one race with a shattered windscreen – another rider had leant so hard on Ivy that he put his shoulder through it.

As far as Tom was concerned, 1965 was not only memorable for its success, it was particularly enjoyable because his riders were such a pleasure to work with and appreciated everything that was done for them. On top of Bill's achievements, Paddy Driver rode some superb races, but his performances were slightly overshadowed by those of his little team-mate, and he didn't really get the recognition he deserved from the public who had eyes only for Ivy. The new hero stood in the limelight, while Paddy stood in the wings, but for Tom, it was Paddy's ungrudging, sporting attitude which made everything complete. Driver had ridden for Kirby for a long time, but he had to take a back seat immediately Bill arrived on the scene. There were no team orders favouring either of the riders – it was a free-for-all – but Bill usually won simply because he was the better rider. Some riders in Driver's position would have been resentful and jealous, but not Paddy who did everything he could to help Bill, encouraging him, passing on the knowledge gained from years of experience, and always quick to back him up if he was having a hard time from other riders on the circuit.

Paddy realised that Bill had something that he never had, and he accepted it. There was no animosity between the two riders at any time, and they struck up a firm friendship. Paddy was known as 'The Clown Prince', because of his jovial, humorous manner. He was a great one for larking about when he wasn't actually racing, and of course, nothing could have suited Bill better. It would be hard to imagine two men more ideally suited to race as a team, and Tom enjoyed their 'performances' in the paddock as much as their efforts on the track. They pulled his leg unmercifully, re-living the experiences encountered in their battles. Bill would relate how he 'did' this rider or that, and Paddy would chime in, 'It's a good thing it happened round the back of the circuit – old Uncle would have had kittens if he'd seen you doing that! By crikey, mate, you took a chance there; it bloody well frightened me sitting behind and *watching* you do it!'

Bill would retaliate. 'Cor! You've got some room to talk – what about *you* when you dived up the inside of the bunch going into Druids!' The pair would exchange such remarks with dead-pan faces, apparently in all seriousness, and then, when they saw poor Uncle's growing expression of alarm they would collapse into helpless laughter. Although there were often 'hairy' moments in the races, the recounting of them was usually done in a light-hearted manner with a lot of jesting, and Paddy, always a great one for telling stories, would describe everything vividly, mimicking all the sound effects of squealing brakes and revving engines. In later years, when Bill had the added responsibilities of a works rider, he said that his days with Uncle Tom and Paddy were the happiest of his life.

Ivy continued to race the Honda for Chisholms', and in the 125cc events he was in a class of his own. But since leaving Monty he had not contested the 250 races, which pleased Tom because it had cut out at least one event from Bill's hectic programme. Then another sponsor, Frank Higley, wanted a rider for his new 250cc Cotton, so he approached Kirby to see if he would allow Bill to consider it. Tom wasn't keen on the idea, and he told Frank that he thought Bill had too much on his plate already, explaining that he had been unable to persuade his rider to concentrate on the big classes, though conceding that Bill seemed to ride just as well whether he did ten races or two. In the end he told Frank that if Bill wanted to ride the Cotton, then he wouldn't stand in his way, and after testing the machine Ivy decided he *would* like to race it. Frank was surprised and delighted, but Tom, while admiring his rider's ability to cope with all four solo events, still felt it was too much, although he was as good as his word and reluctantly agreed.

'Derek Minter was riding the official works Cotton,' Higley explained, 'and my arrangement with the factory was that we would have an identical machine, but when it came ours only had a four-speed gearbox whereas Minter's had a six. Even so, Bill usually managed to stay with Minter, and occasionally beat him. I fought tooth-and-nail to get a six-speeder for Bill. I wrote to the factory and asked them how Bill could possibly compete with Minter when he only had a four-speed gearbox; I said that if ever a rider was worth a six-speeder it was Bill Ivy. We were still pushing for it when some factory officials came along to one of the race meetings. Bill pulled the race off and said, "If *that's* not bloody well worth a six-speed 'box, I don't know what is." After that the gearbox came so quickly that it wasn't true, and this, to me, showed what *they* also thought of Bill for the effort that he was putting in.'

'The Cottons were clumsy things and they didn't handle too well, so we had a lighter frame made to suit Bill's size. This was when he really started to beat Minter, and from that point on it was anybody's race – they would take one another.

'From the onset he struck me as being a damn good two-stroke rider. Although he didn't strike me as being very mechanically minded, he seemed to know *exactly* what was going on underneath him. I'm certain he had a 'feel' for an engine, and he could diagnose a fault very easily. But the thing that impressed me most of all about Bill, right from the start, was his attitude. If the machine wasn't quite 100 per cent it never seemed to worry him. If I thought that the bike wasn't just sharp I'd tell him, and he would say, "We'll have a go." This was always his attitude, and normally he would come out on top; he would give that little bit extra, which probably more than offset the slight disadvantage of the machine not being quite up to scratch. Bill performed so well on this Cotton. He'd come out against far superior machinery, but his riding ability would just out-do them all the time; he was a *must* for a works team.

'Sometimes he would come in and say that he was 'off today', but this was very seldom. To me, he always rode the same race, and he seemed so tireless. He could keep on and on. Where other riders would flop out in the back of a van after a hard race, Bill would get on another bike and go out to the line again. If some of the bigger men took on what he did in one meeting they would have been shattered.'

People do not associate strength with men of small stature, but Ivy was an exception. Undoubtedly, his ability to take on so much lay in his being so strong. Uncle Tom was astounded to see him lift the big Matchless into the van with apparent ease – all by himself.

Whether the secret of Ivy's stamina had anything to do with the vast number of bottles of ice-cream soda he consumed during a meeting, no-one ever knew, but he seemed to drink it by the gallon. On one particularly hot day another rider, seeing Bill guzzling away, asked if he could have a drink. 'Help yourself,' came the reply, so he selected one of the bottles lying on the floor of the van, took a hearty swig – and nearly exploded. He'd picked up the wrong bottle and had drunk a good mouthful of the paint thinners which Bill kept for removing the racing numbers from the bikes!

Motor Circuit Developments, the syndicate which controls four of the most popular motorcycle circuits in England, were delighted with the success of Kirby's new signing, for Ivy had captured the imagination of the fans who swarmed to the meetings to see their idol in action. Consequently, Ivy became 'hot property' to the organisers in the racing world. He was a crowd-puller, and John Webb, head of the MCD organisation, fully appreciated the value of good publicity, so he spoke to Tom Kirby and suggested that it would be an excellent idea if Ivy's image could be promoted further. Tom agreed, and it was decided to promote a 'David and Goliath' image, with Bill as the little 'Giant Killer' from Maidstone.

The Press were very willing to co-operate to ensure maximum publicity, and Radio London, the pirate, sea-based pop station, adopted the Kirby team and plugged them over the air as The Radio London–Kirby team. Curiously, Bill was rather reluctant and apprehensive about the whole scheme to begin with, but he agreed to give it a try. Although he was a flamboyant character, his humour and sense of fun was never planned – it was just spontaneous. He hated contrived practical jokes, and his humour was based on off-the-cuff joviality which thrived on inspirations of the moment. As far as he was concerned, the idea of putting on what he considered to be a planned act for the benefit of the public didn't appeal to him in the least. But Tom explained that he didn't have to put on a big act. 'Just be yourself,' he said, 'and let everyone else do the promotional work.' All he had to do was to meet his public, attend social functions and just be himself, for he was a born showman, although at this stage in his life it probably never occurred to him.

It wasn't long before Ivy entered into the spirit of things. Once he became used to being fussed over, treated as a celebrity, and seeing the public eye for ever being turned in his direction, he really began to enjoy himself and appreciate the value of an audience. In the nicest possible way, he was a show-off who revelled in the attentions of his fans and the 'dollies' who clamoured for his autograph. It became a familiar sight to see Bill larking around in the paddock, surrounded by a crowd of admirers. Sometimes, if he knew people were watching him, he would do something outrageously funny, just to entertain them. If he was a bit stiff after a race, he would come into the paddock and walk up and down on his hands, or turn a few cartwheels to loosen up.

At one meeting, the riders were lined up on the grid, poised for the off, and the starter actually had the flag raised when the silence was broken by a shout, 'STOP!' Needless to say, it was Bill. 'Hang on a tick, mate,' he said, 'can you lend me your flag to wipe my goggles – they've misted up!' Only Ivy's boyish impudence could have got away with it. The other riders laughed, and of course the spectators loved it.

Although Bill was a very easy-going person, he also had a stubborn, argumentative streak. If an issue was involved and he considered himself to be on the right side of it, he would argue heatedly, yet he hated rowing or falling out with anyone. He inherited this from his father, who was equally stubborn, and Mrs Ivy would walk out discreetly into the kitchen when Bill and Ringo got going at home. Although the pair of them thought a lot of each other, they would argue persistently at times, each convinced that his opinion was right and wanting the last word.

Bill had his ups and downs with Uncle, too. Sometimes they would have a flare-up in the paddock, but this, as anyone who has been connected with racing will know, is only to be expected now and again. Even in the pits the atmosphere can be electrifying, especially when the pressure is on. A rider is constantly on edge, and even when he's not actually racing the tension can still be there. Keyed-up and full of nervous energy, it is impossible to relax until the last race has been run. Bill's usual outlet was his sense of humour, but occasionally this would give way to a state of irritation.

D

On the other hand, a sponsor's job is a very demanding one, for he has the responsibilities of the whole organisation on his shoulders. It is his task to ensure that everything runs as smoothly as possible, that everything is checked and double-checked. Riders and mechanics have to be organised, and so do machines; absolutely nothing can be left to chance when a man's life may depend on it.

Each bike is set-up to the rider's preference, to a degree that an outsider to the sport would probably consider unnecessarily finicky. Machines that appear identical are often vastly different. Suspension settings, riding positions, control layout, gear ratios, tyre pressures, and a host of other items vary from one machine to another. Each mount is tailored to the individual requirements of its jockey, and getting a bike set-up so that the rider is really happy with it is a major job in itself, for what is right for one circuit could be totally wrong for another.

Often, a mechanical fault has to be rectified in haste as the precious seconds tick away. Tactics have to be planned, pit signals arranged, lap times recorded, and a dozen other things attended to. A sponsor or team manager requires a cool head and a quick brain, and Tom Kirby has both. Some people in the game have called him 'fussy'. It doesn't matter which adjective is used – call it fussy, call it meticulous – it's the results that count. Kirby has often admitted that he gets 'butterflies' every time one of his bikes goes out to the line.

In the midst of all this tension and drama, it is only natural that a rider and his sponsor occasionally will have words. If Tom and Bill didn't see eye-to-eye over something, they would have it out. If Mrs Ivy went into the paddock and found the pair of them airing their grievances, she would walk away thinking, 'Oh dear, I wish Bill wouldn't speak to Tom like that!' Then, when she returned later, they would be laughing and joking as though nothing had happened. Not that Bill would be rude to his sponsor, but he would emphatically make known his opinion. 'This,' relates Mrs Ivy, 'is why Tom and Bill got on so well. They knew exactly where they stood with each other because they spoke their minds.'

However, Bill's outspokenness sometimes got him into hot water. Tom still remembers when the 'little devil' cost him 10 quid because he couldn't keep a still tongue in his head. Uncle was driving Bill's Jaguar – identical to his own – with the bikes on a trailer hitched behind, and Bill was fast asleep on the back seat as they motored along. Suddenly, a police car appeared from nowhere and gonged them. On stopping, the police officer came over and asked Tom what he thought he was doing, driving so fast. Tom replied that he wasn't breaking the speed limit, but then it was pointed out to him that all vehicles towing trailers were restricted to a maximum of 40 mph. Unaccustomed to pulling trailers, he had forgotten all about it! Tom then began to talk himself out of the sticky situation with a masterpiece of oral strategy (delivered in an extremely polite manner), and in all probability would have escaped with a caution . . . if only Bill had not woken up, summed-up the situation through bleary eyes, assumed wrongly that Uncle was being booked, and decided to tell the copper exactly what he thought of him, which he did, most emphatically. This untimely speech led to a change in the policeman's attitude, and out came his notebook, which resulted in Tom being fined for speeding. He still maintains that if Bill had carried on sleeping he would have been £10 better off!

Ivy and Kirby made an ideal racing partnership, the former's ability and the latter's knowledge of the sport making a formidable combination. They would go down to Brands Hatch between week-ends, testing new ideas on the machines, discussing tactics, experimenting with different techniques, everything being exploited thoroughly to discover if it produced even a fractional improvement. Every aspect of the game was analysed and discussed down to the minutest detail. Bill would experiment with a variety of racing lines, while Tom stood at the trackside with a board full of stopwatches and sheets of foolscap, timing his rider on individual sections and over complete laps, recording everything and looking for vital split-second gains.

At one of these sessions, when Bill first joined Kirby's team, Uncle suggested that if Bill could slightly alter his line, it might enable him to get the power on earlier when accelerating out of the bends. 'I know what you want me to do, Uncle,' Bill replied, '*whack it early and whack it hard!*' Experiments along these lines paid dividends, and Ivy adopted the phrase as one of his favourite expressions.

Unbeaten in his first nine races on the big Matchless, Ivy set his sights on winning the British Championship, and Tom persuaded him to pack up work to concentrate exclusively on his career. Bill was reluctant to leave Chisholms as he still enjoyed working there, but as the demands on his racing grew it was the logical thing to do. What with midweek practising and all the paperwork to contend with, Bill had enough to keep him occupied. Mrs Ivy and Sue assisted with the office work, which included answering a steadily increasing stream of fan mail.

So Ivy left the brothers, Don and Bill, who had set him on the path to success six years previously, and turned professional. He knew how much he owed to the Chisholms, and he never forgot to show his gratitude. Even when he stopped working at the shop, Bill would often pop in to see everybody for a chat.

Despite his dislike of the Isle of Man circuit, which he had the guts openly to admit, Bill knew that he would have to learn to ride it, and ride it well if he was to be successful in world-class racing. 'It scares the bloody pants off me,' he confided to Uncle when they were discussing the forthcoming TT events, which were just a few weeks away. As usual, he had entered all four solo classes, but his knowledge of the arduous 37¾-mile circuit was very limited. Tom advised, 'This is part of the programme that you will have to do if you become a works rider. I'm not expecting you to do great things in the island so don't expect too much yourself. Go out to learn the circuit and we'll accept the positions where you finish.'

Then out of the blue came an offer to test-ride the works Yamahas at Silverstone, with a view to supporting the regular team riders Mike Duff and Phil Read in the Isle of Man and at the Dutch TT. Bill Ivy's big chance had arrived.

4

Yamaha

THE ACTIONS OF both Tom Kirby and Frank Higley had aroused Yamaha's interest. Tom had already recommended Ivy to the factory, and Frank, realising just how quickly Bill would go on a really top-class 250, had written to the Japanese company's Dutch base stating that he was prepared to purchase the best racing machine they could sell him, *price no object*, and that he intended to put Bill Ivy on it. Obviously such a display of confidence could not be ignored, and the Japanese were intrigued, so they invited Ivy to Silverstone to find out just how good he was.

Phil Read, 250cc World Champion and captain of the Yamaha team, also nominated Bill and did all he could to help his chances. It was obvious that he wanted Bill in the team, and this undoubtedly influenced Yamahas who, after seeing him perform well in his tests, selected him to contest both the Isle of Man and the Dutch world championship rounds.

Unfortunately, Bill could not have had a worse circuit on which to make his works début. He was really thrilled about being offered the bikes, but he was also very concerned about how well he would perform on them in the Island. If it had been anywhere else he would have been confident, but as he hardly knew his way round the TT course he was more than a little apprehensive. There would be no chance to take things easy on the works bikes – too much was at stake – so his former plan had to be scrapped. This was his big chance, so he *had* to do well, even though the competition would be of the highest possible standard. In his biggest challenge yet he would be competing against the world's best; men who knew the treacherous, demanding circuit like their own back gardens, and were mounted on the fastest racing motorcycles in existence.

Plucky little Ivy need not have worried, for he certainly didn't disgrace himself on Mona's fickle isle. Although Lady Luck declined to ride on his shoulder for the greater part of the week he gained a moral victory in spite of receiving the chequered flag only once. He frightened himself repeatedly, had abominably cruel luck, threw himself down the road once, yet reaped the glory on sheer effort alone. He proved himself as a competent works rider, and displayed all the qualities of a future World Champion.

The knowing ones shook their heads as they watched the diminutive rider fling the Yamahas round the mountain circuit with a distinct lack of finesse. Ivy's riding was described by some as downright dangerous, but how many spectators realised that he was relying solely on his courage and every ounce of natural skill that he possessed, to offset his inferior knowledge of the course?

In his first event of the week, the Lightweight 250cc race, Bill put up an incredible performance by lapping at over 98 mph – only 2 mph slower than the new lap record set by Phil Read on the opening lap. Read led during the initial stages and established a useful lead over the Honda team captain, Jim Redman, his wily arch-rival from Rhodesia, as Bill ran third. Then Phil retired on the second lap, which hoisted Ivy into second place, 30 seconds behind Redman and almost a full minute ahead of team-mate Mike Duff. There were odd patches of mist on the mountain, making visibility poor, and Bill confused the left-hander at Brandy-well with a similar section, got off line and down he went. Although he was unscathed, one of the carburettors was damaged, so Bill had no alternative but to retire. Bitterly disappointed, he pushed his battered Yamaha back to the pits to receive a tremendous ovation from the crowds in the grandstand.

He fared no better in the 350cc Junior event on Uncle's 7R AJS. Despite an excursion up the slip road at Creg-ny-Baa (due to braking too late) he was holding eighth place, but retired on the fifth lap with a broken chain.

Ivy faced his toughest opposition in the Ultra-Lightweight 125cc event, for works teams were also being fielded by Japanese rivals Honda and Suzuki, and the East German MZ concern. This was the only race he completed during the whole week. Riding one of the older air-cooled Yamahas, Bill came home seventh at over 90 mph in a closely fought race which clinched the manufacturers' team award for Yamaha, with Read winning and Duff finishing third, both of them on the new water-cooled models.

In appalling conditions (which brought down both Mike Hail-wood and his MV team-mate Giacomo Agostini) Bill retired in the

Senior 500cc race on the second lap with a split crankcase on the Kirby-Matchless. Hailwood climbed back on his bent bike and still won.

In the face of these set-backs and disappointments Ivy caused a sensation in his first outings on the Yamahas, especially for his superb showing on the bigger of the flying two-stokes. In a Press interview afterwards he admitted that he'd had an anxious moment at virtually every corner, 'because I was trying so hard'. He went on to recount an alarming incident which occurred during practice:

'I had one particularly nasty moment at the top of Bray Hill. I was going through flat-out on the 250 when the rear wheel left the ground on a little bump. The revs soared and when the wheel hit the ground again the front-end reared up. Phew! I shut down after that.

'Although two-stroke engines have a reputation for seizing, you never think yours is going to, but if it does you just have to be ready. During practice the smaller Yamaha seized at the end of the Sulby Straight, and the 250 at an almost flat-out left-hander near Rhencullen. Fortunately, I whipped the clutch in quickly enough on each occasion.'

Bill admitted that he was nervous of the ultra-fast works machines, and he was very conscious of his limited knowledge of the circuit. Also, because of his light weight he found the big Yamaha a handful on the rough sections – the bike jumped all over the place.

There is little time for relaxation during the fatiguing TT schedule. Not only is race week itself very tiring, but so is the previous practice week, which necessitates rising at 4.30 am for the dawn training sessions when the roads are closed (the course is run over public highways which are usually open to everyday traffic). But to anyone who has not visited this picturesque island gem, it is difficult to describe the atmosphere which exists there during TT time. There is nothing remotely like it anywhere else in the world. To lie in bed in the mornings, listening to the open exhausts of the racing machines burbling their way along the promenade and up the hill to the starting area; to throw open the hotel window and sniff the bracing sea air, tinged with the faint odour of burnt racing oil; to gaze at hundreds of enthusiasts' machines parked in regiments along the Douglas sea-front, glistening in the early morning sunlight; for thousands of fans this is all part of their annual pilgrimage and holiday. But for anyone connected with the racing the

TT means a fortnight of hard work, after which a break would be very welcome instead of the mad scramble to catch the boat to Liverpool and on to Mallory Park, immediately after the Senior race on the Friday. Saturday is usually spent sorting-out the bikes, and it is a familiar sight to see mechanics working furiously, completely dismantling machines in an effort to get them ready for the Post-TT International the following day.

Back on the familiar ground of Mallory Park, Ivy was in devastating form. He won the 125cc race, was second to Redman's works Honda in the 350cc event, and did the seemingly impossible in the 500cc skirmish by leading the great Mike Hailwood for the first six laps on a vastly inferior machine. Bill thrust his single-cylinder Matchless to the front, with Mike in his wake, the scarlet MV wailing its battle-cry out of the four exhausts. The champion wasn't playing cat-and-mouse, either, for the rising star from Kent was making him fight every inch of the way. But gradually Hailwood's superior speed and experience told, and he edged past at the Esses and went on to win by 200 yards. Afterwards, he admitted that he had really been trying, and with typical modesty said, 'I think Bill let me win – actually, I think he could have won it'. Mike insisted that Bill should accompany him on the lap of honour, and after being presented with the victor's laurels, he promptly placed them around Ivy's shoulders and made him lead on the customary tour of the circuit. This sporting gesture was enthusiastically received by the delighted crowds, who gave the two riders a tremendous ovation. The motorcycling Press dubbed Bill as 'a giant at Mallory'.

Mike had first seen Bill several years previously, on what he described as 'those Itom things'. Then he began to take notice when Ivy rode the Monards because, like everyone else he was intrigued to see such a small chap on a big bike. 'But he used to send them along a bit, didn't he!', said Mike.

By this time the two riders had formed a firm friendship, and Bill spent more time at Mike's flat, on the outskirts of London, than he did at home. Although he never adopted a defeatist attitude when competing against the maestro Bill always said of Mike, 'He's the greatest, and whether he wins or loses he always smiles'. He told his mother that he could never hope to be as good as Mike – nobody could. 'The best I can hope for is to try to be better than all the others.' Ivy maintained this right through his career. Even though he beat the champion of champions on occasions, he always regarded Hailwood as being head-and-shoulders above everyone else, including himself, and he showed his respect by nicknaming Mike 'Ace'.

After Mallory it was on to Assen, the home of the Dutch TT, the next weekend. Bill caused considerable hilarity at the weigh-in on practice day. The stipulated minimum weight ruling for a rider is 9 stones 6 pounds, and 'officially' this was Ivy's exact weight. But in fact, he only weighed just 9 stone, and when he stood on the scales the official in charge would not pass him. Bill was instructed to get his helmet and boots, then weigh himself again with these on the scales. He returned with them, jumped on the scales again, and to the official's utter astonishment the little chap was now 4 pounds *over* the minimum. He scratched his head, shrugged his shoulders and recorded the figures in his book, as Bill shot away chuckling mischievously – he had concealed rear chains in his helmet and riding boots!

Six seconds slower than the Suzuki of pace-setter Hugh Anderson in practice, Ivy was again at a disadvantage as it was his first visit to the twisty five-miles circuit. Furthermore, his older 125cc works Yamaha was no match for the new water-cooled models, or the new Suzukis, but he still finished a creditable fourth. He latched on to Anderson, the current 125cc World Champion and Suzuki captain, early in the race, slipstreaming him down the straights and 'picking his brains' round the corners. This enabled Bill to catch the leaders, and he finished 13 seconds behind the winner, Mike Duff, and the Suzukis of Anderson and Yoshima Katayama, the fiery Japanese rider.

In the 500cc race, Ivy held a magnificent third place behind the MVs of Hailwood and Agostini, and had the latter in sight until he was forced to drop back when a plug lead came adrift; finally he retired when the gearbox packed up.

Back in the paddock the Japanese Yamaha mechanics, helpful as ever, were struggling to put the big Matchless on the stand, and when Bill saw what was going on, he calmly hoisted the back end into the air and kicked the stand under the bike with his foot. The little Nipponese men just stood and gaped, for Ivy was smaller than most of them.

Bill was very popular with the whole Japanese contingent who took an immediate liking to him and quickly named him 'Ivy-San'. To add 'San' after a person's name is a Japanese custom showing friendship and respect. They enjoyed having Ivy-San in the team, and would look on, grinning hugely in obvious delight at his amusing antics.

After giving his very best at the TT and in Holland, Ivy's spell
on the Yamahas came to an end, and there began an agonising
season-long wait to see if the Japanese would again call on his
services. He wondered whether he had come up to their expecta-
tions. Did they think he was good enough? Had he ridden well
enough to impress them as a possible candidate for a regular place
in the team? His races on the Yamahas had whetted his appetite,
and he was keener than ever to become a fully fledged works rider
and join the gladiators of the grand prix arenas. But it was no good
worrying about it, only time would tell. In the meantime, it was
back to the British short circuits to face the home challenge.

During the meetings which followed, poor Derek Minter's ego
took a severe knock, not only at Ivy's capable hands, but also by
the Press, who were inclined to rub it in a bit as well. Minter had
been the undisputed King of the home tracks, although John
Cooper managed to beat him occasionally, but immediately Ivy got
astride Kirby's bikes the crowds had a new hero, and there was
very little Minter could do about it. In the 500cc class Ivy was
virtually invincible, but he was not as successful on the 350, and
Derek usually claimed back some of his lost glory by winning this
class. The thing which really hurt Minter was the fact that he had
advised Bill to try to get into the Kirby team – a piece of advice
that later he was to regret over and over again.

'No champion likes to be beaten,' revealed the man they rightly
named 'The Kentish Flyer'. 'Bill and I were good friends, and it
wasn't until we got to the starting line ... I'm not saying we were
enemies, but you've got no friends then – you're out to win! I
suppose you could say that a little bit of a needle developed
between us.'

Understandably, Minter was as determined to hang on to the
500cc British title, as Ivy was determined to wrest it from him.
'IVY BRANDS THE MINT' and 'BILL IVY TILTS MIN-
TER'S CROWN' were among the headlines that added to the
reigning champion's humiliation, and spurred him into scintillat-
ing action when the big day came at Oulton Park. Derek was
always at his best at the Cheshire circuit – it was one of his
favourites – and Bill knew that he would have to ride like a demon
to win the race and the title that went with it.

When the flag dropped, Derek made one of his notoriously bad
getaways, and as he set about carving his way through the pack
Ivy established a good lead. But Minter was in no mood to accept
defeat. Riding with all his old dash he narrowed the gap relentlessly

between his Petty-tuned Norton and the flying Kirby-Matchless. For the final laps, the champ and the challenger had the crowd on their toes with their cut-and-thrust riding. It seemed to be anyone's race, but although Derek had ridden magnificently to catch Bill, try as he might he just couldn't get past; every move was blocked, every manoeuvre anticipated and countered. As the two machines thundered across the line Ivy got the verdict by the narrowest of margins; the giant-killer had done it again, and Britain had a new 500cc champion.

While the victor went to collect his spoils and receive the acclaim of the crowd, a dejected Minter stormed back to the paddock, bitterly complaining that Ivy had ridden dirty. When Bill returned to the paddock, grinning wide and proudly bearing an armful of trophies, the smile was quickly wiped off his face by Derek's angry remarks. Fortunately, Uncle Tom took charge of the situation. 'Go and put your trophies in the car, Bill,' he said, '*I'll* sort this out!' With that, he stomped over to Derek, 'What's all this I hear about you accusing Bill of riding dirty?' Derek began to voice his protests, but Tom cut him short. 'Look,' he said, 'Bill beat you fair and square – he was the better man on the day – and if he rode dirty, *you bloody well taught him!*' With this scathing remark, Tom turned on his heel and walked away.

Here, the reader must not get the wrong impression of Derek Minter, for he certainly wasn't a bad sportsman. This incident has been included merely to illustrate that racing is not all glamour and that sometimes the tension, frustration, and bitter disappointment cause a rider to give vent to his feelings in the heat of the moment. Nerves, stretched to breaking point, can suddenly snap, and when there is so much at stake, a rider becomes even more highly strung and sensitive. An occasional angry outburst, and a few odd incidents of controversy are inevitable, but they are soon forgotten. Defeat is a hard pill to swallow after years of superiority, and Minter had been a fine champion, and still had several good years' riding in front of him at that stage of his career, even though his days of complete domination had ended. In all probability, Bill had beaten Derek by *forceful* riding, but if the opportunity had presented itself, Minter surely would have used precisely the same tactics to have remained in front.

As the Kirby team had agreed to fit in with MCD's promotional plans, they were allowed to go testing at Brands Hatch almost at will. Through popping down to the Kentish circuit so frequently, Tom and Bill soon became acquainted with the boys who ran the racing drivers' school there, and Geoff Clarke of Motor Racing Stables and Tony Lanfranchi, his chief instructor, soon became friends with the motorcycling pair.

Ivy had wanted to have a go round the track in a single-seater racing car for a long time as the idea of hurtling round on four wheels appealed to him, so it was inevitable that he should raise the subject with Geoff and Tony. A lesson was duly arranged, and so the familiar surroundings of Brands Hatch once again witnessed an Ivy début, as they had seven years previously. But this time it was a very different Bill Ivy. The boy had grown into a young man; the novice into a champion; and the 50cc motorcycle had been forsaken long ago and in its place on this occasion was a sleek, powerful racing car. The only similarity was the potential shown by the performer. Just as Charlie Surridge had nodded his head in approval at the boy on the Itom, so did Geoff and Tony as they watched Ivy hurl the car round the track with a natural skill that made a mockery of his complete lack of experience on four wheels.

Obviously, Bill lacked polish, but that natural aptitude to control anything on wheels at speed, that abundance of inborn ability, and that tremendous will to succeed all shone through. Nobody had expected anything extraordinary, but Ivy showed amazing promise by quickly adapting to the vastly different technique of handling a racing car. He put up some incredible lap times for a first-time effort, and this initial step was to be the beginning of another chapter in his life of speed. His interest aroused, his appetite whetted, Bill decided to take up the challenge of motor racing and to compete in the occasional race whenever his motorcycle commitments allowed. So he signed-up for a complete course of instruction at the school, practised hard, and learnt as much about racing cars as he could.

At his first car meeting, at Brands Hatch, Bill felt a bit like a fish out of water. Although the venue was the same, it seemed like a different world, with different people, a different 'lingo', and a strange new atmosphere. Ivy had created a lot of interest among the car people, but he felt slightly embarrassed about it. He missed the familiar faces of his motorcycle rivals and the good-natured bantering from the people he knew. He knew hardly any of the car drivers, and although they seemed friendly enough he still felt a stranger among them. He even declined to put on his new racing overalls until Uncle Tom arrived because he felt rather conspicuous in them. However, with Uncle there to encourage him, Bill felt a lot happier and he went out for his race, spun off the track at Clearways due to over-enthusiasm, and got back into the race to finish a very creditable fifth.

'Bill came to us originally,' relates Geoff Clarke, 'just for a run round in a single-seater, as quite a few of the top motorcyclists have done. Some of them have "stuffed" the cars and may remain nameless, but Ivy showed tremendous flair right from the start. Mind you, he used to spin a lot at first, and he did crash occasionally, but he seemed to be completely fearless. It didn't worry him if he spun off or anything. He was a really 'gutsy' little character and he had a terrific amount of determination. I can remember two incidents (nothing to do with his racing), when Bill's determination really impressed me.

'One evening a crowd of us were in the bar at the "Hilltops", a club near Brands patronised by a lot of the racing personalities, when a topic came up during conversation as to how many "press-ups" one could do. Most of the chaps sitting around said, "Oh, I could do . . . 15." Somebody else said, "20", then when Bill said, "You could do more than that!" another person challenged him. "Well, Bill, you couldn't do 50, that's for sure!" Quick as a flash Bill replied, "I could".

'So bets were laid as to whether Bill could do 50 press-ups or not, and I backed him for a fiver. I didn't know whether he could or not, but I thought that if Bill said he could do 50 he would *do* 50. Now, 50 press-ups is an awful lot – a hell of a number.

'Anyway, the bets were laid and old Bill got down on the carpet, and I should think the first 30 or 40 were really done at speed; he must have been in training because he was incredibly fit. Having rattled off these quick ones, his back as straight as a rod, he slowed down to the speed at which most people would start, worked his way up to 48 then 49 . . . and after a bit of a psychological hurdle just managed the last one. It had taken a supreme effort, but he made it. Of course I won my £5, and everybody clapped him on the back; poor Bill was absolutely exhausted, but happy!

'I'll give you another example of his gutsy character which also took place at the "Hilltops". On this occasion the subject was how quickly one could run from the club to the main gates of Brands and back again. The question had arisen from an earlier discussion we'd had at the racing school regarding how quickly one could run round the short circuit. We had one chap who fancied himself as a long-distance runner, and bets were laid between him and Bill as to who would win a race to Brands and back (a distance of three or four miles).

'Everybody watched the two runners as they set off jog-trotting down the road at about midnight, and after a while, Tony and I followed in the car to see how they were getting on. They had just reached the main gates, had turned round and were coming back, so we went back to the club, had another drink and went out again to see who was winning. About a quarter of a mile down the road there was Bill virtually carrying this other chap. He'd won the race because his rival had given up, and Bill was actually carrying the exhausted fellow in. He really was a tremendous little chap.'

Ivy continued to compete in a few more car races during 1965, and Motor Racing Stables were so impressed that they supplied him with a car and entered him under the school banner. He advanced so much that he was even engaged as an instructor at the school. In a Formula 3 car he was capable of lapping within half a second of the lap record on the short circuit, and within one second on the grand prix circuit – it was almost unbelievable.

When Bill finished riding the Chis-Honda, (he virtually handed it over to Roy Francis because he knew that he could get hold of another machine) he contacted Bill Hannah, the Liverpool sponsor. Hannah promised to loan Bill his Honda, provided he was prepared to do all the work on it himself. It was the bike which Chris Vincent had used, and Hannah explained that it had done a lot of races, was in rather a state, and that Bill would have to put it right before racing it. So he collected the bike, took it home and completely dismantled it. This was on a Saturday, and Bill was supposed to be riding it at Brands the following day. When Mrs Ivy saw what a state the bike was in, and her son standing in the middle of piles of bits strewn all over the lawn, she said, 'You'll *never* race *that!*'

'I will,' Bill replied, confidently. But his mother was convinced that he would never get the machine together and running properly in time, for it looked to be in very bad condition. 'Well, you won't do any good on it,' she said with conviction. Bill shrugged his shoulders. 'I will, you know. It's a Honda isn't it, a standard racing Honda the same as the other one?'

Mrs Ivy had to smile, for Bill screwed the bike together, took it up to Brands and still won on it just the same. 'There you are, Ethel,' he said, 'I told you,' (with extreme satisfaction) 'it's a Honda, and if you put them together right, one is as good as another.'

The final motorcycle meeting at Brands Hatch that year was the *Evening News*-sponsored Race of the South, and what a magnificent finale it was. Mike Hailwood joined forces with the Kirby team, and after practice the three riders were having a chat with Uncle Tom in the clubhouse. Bill turned to Mike, and with his typical impish grin said, 'Well, you've had it today, mate – Paddy and I are out to beat you!' With that, all three riders looked at Tom. 'Well lads,' he said, 'you're all going out there to do your best. We don't want anything stupid going on . . . just put on a good show and let the best man win!' Nothing could have suited the trio better, 'That's all we wanted to know . . . that's great,' they all chorused. Mike knew that his team-mates would really be gunning for him.

Hailwood's attitude never failed to impress Kirby, for he never adopted the 'I'm the champion – give me the bikes – I'm going out to show 'em' attitude. Whenever he rode for Tom Mike always asked what was expected of him, and what he could rev the bikes to, and he never forgot to show his gratitude for being provided with machines when the MV wasn't available for short-circuit meetings.

There was no power advantage in the champion's favour this time, for he and Bill were on identical machines. In the 500cc race, Bill *did* beat Mike, but 'Ace' fell off round Druids, due to what Tom described as 'larking about and looking round to see where Bill was half-way round the corner!' So the chips were really down for the big event, the 1,000cc Race of the South. The friendly rivals fought it out for the entire 20 laps, and Ivy seemed certain of victory as he sped into the last bend on the final lap, leading by a machine's length. Then Mike showed precisely why he earned 'the greatest' tag, by diving through and snatching victory from under Bill's nose. There was no more than a yard in it, but Mike was the winner. By finishing in third place, Paddy Driver completed a fine 1 – 2 – 3 for the Kirby team, and this was the only time a private team had ever bagged the first three places in a British International. Tom was delighted, and to this day he regards this success as his proudest moment in over 20 years of racing.

On Friday, October 15, 1965, around 11 o'clock in the morning, the telephone rang in the Ivys' home. Mrs Ivy took the call, and as usual it was for Bill, although he was at Brands Hatch, practising in a car. 'Can I take a message?' she inquired. The voice had sounded urgent, but when Mrs Ivy learnt that it was Yamaha, Tokyo, on the other end of the line, and that they wanted Bill to fly out to Japan for the Grand Prix, she could hardly believe her ears. The unlucky Canadian, Mike Duff, had injured himself in a training spill and would not be fit for the race, so Yamahas wanted Ivy-San as a replacement.

She took down all the details and phoned Brands Hatch. Bill was out on the circuit, but a marshal flagged him down, 'Quick, you're wanted on the phone, Bill – it's *urgent*!' Scrambling out of the car and running across the paddock, Bill wondered what it could be – he hoped it wasn't bad news. He reached the telephone rather breathlessly, but the anxious frown soon disappeared as his mother told him the news. 'Yamaha have phoned – all the way from Japan,' she told him excitedly, 'they want you to fly out there for the Grand Prix!' Bill was elated, 'When?', he asked. 'Immediately!', came the reply.

He dashed home, and the following 24 hours were one mad rush. With the help of his mother, his doctor, the local council, and his brother-in-law, who dashed around to get the vaccine for Bill's inoculation, everything was organised and the necessary documents were obtained in time. Ivy then dashed up to London Airport to catch the plane. He had never flown before, and was rather apprehensive about it; he also worried about whether he would be good enough to take Duff's place in the team. But Mrs Ivy managed to reassure him, and Uncle Tom said, 'You just go out there and ride exactly as you have been riding, and you won't disappoint anybody – including yourself.'

From London to Copenhagen, on to Alaska, and over the North Pole to the land of the rising sun. Bill was tremendously excited, but the flight seemed to drag on for ever until eventually they touched down in Tokyo late on Sunday night. Yamaha officials met Bill and whisked him off to Yokkaichi, near the Suzuka circuit, where they arrived in the early hours of Monday. The Japanese were very friendly towards the little Englishman, and he was booked into a plush hotel and spent the next few hours in welcome slumber; he hadn't slept a wink on the plane. Yamaha's certainly didn't waste any time, for they had their rider out practising that same afternoon, and Ivy's unanticipated arrival caused considerable surprise in the rival Honda and Suzuki camps.

Honda had brought out new machines, five-cylinder 125cc four-strokes which were masterpieces of precision engineering and incredibly quick. The smaller Yamahas were outpaced, but Ivy clinched fourth place in the 125cc event, behind Anderson's Suzuki and the Hondas of Luigi Taveri, the brilliant Swiss rider, and Ulsterman Ralph Bryans.

In the 250cc race, watched by an estimated 80,000 strong crowd,

Hailwood screamed his Honda-six into an unassailable lead; it was his first race for the Japanese concern after leaving the Italian MV Agusta team. Yamahas had their new water-cooled four-cylinder two-strokes for both Ivy and Read, but it was a disastrous race for Read; he slid off on the first lap, while Ivy's bike oiled its plugs at the start. After a quick plug change Bill tore through the pack to finish third behind the Hondas of Hailwood and I. Kasuya.

It was after this race that Mike Hailwood made his classic remark, which had the Europeans chortling with amusement and the Honda officials red-faced with embarrassment. In an interview he was asked what he thought of the new Honda. 'Bloody awful!', Mike replied bluntly, because the bike had handled so badly, even though he had been able to win the race by over two minutes.

Yamaha's must have been impressed with Bill's efforts, for when he flew home he had a works contract in his pocket. Now he was one of the élite band of highly paid factory riders, and would contest both 125 and 250cc classes in all the 1966 world championship rounds. The contract did not allow him to ride for anyone else apart from Tom Kirby, which meant that Bill would no longer be able to race the Hannah-Honda or the Higley-Cotton. He was also restricted to motorcycles, so the motor-racing plans had to be shelved, at least for the time being.

When Ivy returned home, he said, 'The new 250cc Yamaha is so powerful that when you "squirt" it the front wheel comes off the ground.'

He won the final 500cc race of the English season at a rain-soaked Mallory Park, but it almost ended in disaster. Caught-up in a multiple pile-up on the notorious Devil's Elbow, Bill performed what *Motor Cycle News* described as 'a riding miracle' to avoid Marty Lunde, the American rider, and his fallen AJS. Marty had crashed right under Ivy's front wheel.

One week later, that same newspaper published the results of its annual 'Man of the Year' poll. The readers are given the opportunity to vote for the man they consider to be the most outstanding, in any branch of motorcycle sport. To his great surprise and delight, Bill Ivy came out tops, proving just how popular he was by pushing no less a person than Mike Hailwood into second spot, and finishing well in front of Phil Read, Giacomo Agostini, Derek Minter and John Cooper, as well as moto-cross stars Jeff Smith and Dave Bickers.

E

For Bill, this was a highlight in his life, and provided the crowning glory to a superb season. He had won both 125 and 500cc AC-U Stars; the 500cc British Championship; the Brands Hatch Shield; earned himself a place in the Yamaha team; and on top of all that was 'Man of the Year' as well. Few, if any, years could have given him more satisfaction than 1965, for this was the turning point in his career.

5

Service and courage

BEING SUCCESSFUL had its rewards, for it enabled Bill to buy and do things which otherwise he could never have afforded. With his love of fast cars, it was only to be expected that he would spend some of his hard-earned cash on a sports car, so the old Jaguar was replaced by a gleaming E-type, which proved to be an even better 'dollie-puller' than its predecessor.

His liking for speed and thrills expanded into a new sphere when he took up flying as a hobby. Whether his first flight to Japan had influenced him, or whether it was because Phil Read and Mike Hailwood were both keen pilots it's difficult to say, but Bill joined the motorcycling jet-set by taking a course of lessons at Biggin Hill airfield.

He didn't throw his money around, but he believed in having a good time. He enjoyed driving his nice car and he enjoyed zooming around in a light aircraft, but most of all he liked exploring the London night life with Mike Hailwood, who knew all the ropes. A professional rider works extremely hard during the racing season, and by the time Winter arrives he is more than ready for some relaxation and pleasure. But even so, there was still some work to do, testing and developing the machines in readiness for the following year.

Ivy was very much involved in the new Kirby-Rickman project. The Kirby stable and the Rickman brothers, Derek and Don, were working on a completely redesigned set of cycle parts for the AJS and Matchless engines. This involved a lot of hard work, but the enthusiastic little band produced the first prototype within six weeks of completing the drawings and the finalised specification. Named Metisse (French for mongrel), the new frame kits re-styled the Kirby racers into lower, narrower, and lighter machines. As Paddy Driver had retired and gone back to his native South Africa, and Alan Barnett, the new member of the team, hadn't sufficient experience for development test riding, the task of proving the new bikes rested on Ivy's shoulders alone.

The 'marriage' was an immediate success, for the new 500cc Kirby-Metisse made a winning début in the 1966 season-opener at Mallory Park. In Ivy's capable hands the bike won both its heat and the final at record speeds.

Everyone was delighted, and Kirby decided to install his special new short-stroke engine in one of the Metisse layouts. This engine was the brainchild of Jack Williams, formerly the AMC race chief, who had designed the 7R AJS back in the Fifties. Although based on the 7R, the engine incorporated Williams' ideas, and he and Kirby had worked together on the project since its innovation. After a lot of initial teething troubles had been ironed-out, the one-off special was found to produce far more power than the standard 7R unit, and when Ivy tested it in the Metisse frame he was favourably impressed. It was then decided that the bike was ready to race.

In a 350cc heat at Snetterton, it seemed as if the smaller mongrel was also destined to a winning début, for Bill was leading comfortably, but then he came an almighty purler at the Esses. It was a bad one, too, for he was rushed to hospital with a suspected leg fracture, and Tom spent a very anxious time awaiting the results of the doctor's examination. He was very relieved when told that Bill had no bones broken, but the ligaments of his leg had been torn badly, and he was covered in cuts and bruises.

Bill was detained in hospital, and it was a very apologetic sponsor who visited him and explained that the accident had occurred due to the failure of an oil pipe. Unknown to Bill, oil had leaked out all over his rear tyre, and as he cranked the machine over into the corner it had just slid away from underneath him – he hadn't stood a chance. It worried Uncle, because there was no logical reason why the pipe should have fractured; it was brand new and identical to that used on the 500, which had given no trouble at all. Could it be that there were still problems in the new engine?

The pair discussed everything in detail, and the only theory they could think of was that the trouble lay in the oil-housing system. On the Metisse layout the oil tanks had been dispensed with in favour of carrying the oil in the frame tubes. So it was decided to revert to a conventional system and have oil tanks fitted to both machines. But somehow Tom didn't think that this was the complete answer.

'Don't worry, Uncle, you'll find the answer – and as soon as I can get out of this place we can go testing again.' Battered and bruised though he was, all Bill wanted to do was get back on the bike and try to sort out the problem, even though he knew that he could get flung off again. Oil is the motorcyclist's biggest fear. One small patch of it on the track, one smear of it on the tyre, and the consequences can be disastrous; the rider doesn't stand a chance of staying on board, for the moment the machine is heeled over he's off. It's as lethal as riding over a patch of ice.

Uncle admired Bill's plucky attitude, and it was reassuring to have a rider who had so much faith in him. Bill's words kept ringing in his ears, 'You'll find the answer. . . .,' but Uncle was still very worried, for although he racked his brains the answer eluded him.

Both machines were fitted with oil tanks for the Easter meetings, and Bill, stiff and still in pain from his injuries, won the hearts of the Brands Hatch crowd by finishing second to Hailwood's Honda on the 350cc short-stroke, and beating the champion in the big race to win the coveted 'King of Brands' title. Neither Kirby-Metisse gave any trouble during the whole Easter series, and thankfully the problem on the 350 seemed to have disappeared. Everybody concluded that the oil-in-the-frame system must have been at fault, but the reason why remained a complete mystery.

The Easter Sunday meeting at Snetterton produced the most fantastic scenes ever witnessed at the Norfolk circuit. Rain began falling shortly before the start of the 350cc final, and when the field streaked away the circuit was quite wet. Peter Williams, son of Jack the designer, grabbed the lead on the opening lap, and as he sped up the home straight for the first time, Mike Hailwood shot round Russell Bend on his backside. Russell, a slow bottom-gear corner preceding the straight, had been only just added, and the new surface was lethal. As Mike bent down to pick up his fallen Honda two more riders cannoned into him, and the fiasco continued for four laps with riders falling every time round, despite heeding the marshals' waving yellow flags and treating the bend with the utmost respect. No fewer than eight riders came to grief, and men and machines were scattered everywhere, but fortunately nobody was injured. Williams was apparently unperturbed by the surrounding chaos, for he tore round in effortless style, building up a colossal lead until the race was stopped at the end of the fourth lap. Even Derek Minter had pulled-in at the end of the third lap, having seen too many people on their ears. Bill was in second place, miles behind the leader through heeding frantic 'slow down' signals given by Uncle Tom every time he passed the pits.

Although the organisers suggested re-running the race, Hailwood wouldn't hear of competing again. He said that he'd had his chance and had fallen off, so in his opinion a re-run would have been unfair to those riders who had stayed on and were well placed. Most of the others who had crashed agreed, so the positions held at the end of lap four were taken as the finishing order and Peter Williams was declared the winner, but he didn't get the glory or recognition he deserved for his first International victory. After all the drama everyone seemed to have forgotten that Peter had been leading the race by a substantial margin *before* all the others had crashed.

After Easter, Bill dashed off to Spain for the first round of the world championships, held on the tricky Montjuich Park circuit in Barcelona. Both he and Phil had flown out to Japan to test the new Yamahas in March, and both riders had been impressed. Fate smiled upon Bill in the 125cc race, and he scored a great morale-booster by winning from Taveri and Bryans on the Hondas, with Phil finishing fourth. Both retired in the 250 race.

In the West German Grand Prix Bill failed to score due to machine trouble, but at the Dutch TT he took another victory over Luigi Taveri. However, the likeable little Swiss rider was an experienced and wily opponent, and he gained valuable points by winning both the East German and Czechoslovakian rounds while Ivy finished third in each.

At the Finnish round it was Read's turn, and he won from Taveri while Bill failed to score. At this stage, Taveri led the 125cc title chase with three wins and three seconds, Ivy was next with two first places and two thirds, followed by Read with one first, two thirds, and two fourth places. If Ivy was to keep his championship hopes alive he had to do well in the Ulster Grand Prix.

Before going to Ireland, it was back to England again for the Hutchinson 100 meeting. This historical event was to be run at Brands Hatch for the first time, and to retain its unique character, it was decided to run the races in the reverse direction. The Press dubbed the event 'back-to-front Brands', and it was a great success, although for Ivy it was disastrous.

During the first few laps of the 350cc race he was well up the field, and the special short-stroke engine was performing beautifully. Then fate struck again. Rounding South Bank Bend at around 70 mph the bike suddenly shot away from underneath him, and as rider and machine cartwheeled off the track into an advertisement hoarding the other riders gingerly picked their way round the thin black line of oil left by the Kirby-Metisse . . . another oil pipe had gone.

Ivy was taken to hospital without regaining consciousness. He had a badly lacerated back, multiple cuts and bruises, a black eye, and severe concussion . . . and the vital Ulster GP was just one week away.

Ironically, it was to have been Bill's last race for Uncle, for it was written into his contract that he was to cease riding for Kirby once the TT arrived. There was also a clause in the contract which stated that if Bill should fail to honour his commitments with Yamaha due to injury received on Kirby's machines, then both he and Uncle would have to pay Yamaha £200 each for every Grand Prix that was missed.

When Ivy regained consciousness he felt very ill, and was in a great deal of pain, but all he could think about was getting out to Ireland for the race. The doctors told him to forget about it, and said that it was unlikely that he would be fit in time for the TT. But Bill told his mother when she visited him, 'Pack my bags and get my tickets, Ethel – *I'll be on that plane tomorrow.*' Mrs Ivy knew it was useless trying to argue; once Bill had made up his mind you could argue until you ran out of breath, but it wouldn't make any difference.

'I don't want Tom to have to pay out £200 just because I have to miss a race through a few bruises, and I can't let Yamaha down. This meeting is vital to our championship chances, and I *must* ride.' Despite warnings, protests, and sound advice from the medical profession, Ivy discharged himself from hospital. 'I can walk, can't I ?', he told them, 'And if I can walk, I can ride.' But he was in agony, and his head ached fit to burst. Even to walk took every ounce of his courage, and every step was a challenge. His head swam, his vision was blurred, and the stitches in his back pulled every time he moved. But puffed, swollen, and black-and-blue all over, except for his face which was deathly white, somehow Ivy made his way to the airport and boarded the plane.

When the white-faced, battered little figure turned up in Ireland (to the astonishment of everyone), Mr Hasegawa, the Yamaha team manager, took one look at Bill and *ordered* him not to ride, for he was obviously in a bad way. But the Yamaha people were so impressed with their rider's effort and determination that they waived the £200 forfeit, and because Uncle had helped them so much he, too, was told to forget about paying the 'fine'.

In a telephone call to his parents, Bill said, 'I'm here and I feel lousy.' He went on to say that the last thing he remembered was riding round Brands, and that he hadn't the vaguest idea of how he got to Ireland. He admitted that he couldn't remember the accident, being taken to hospital, spending two days there, and then discharging himself and catching the plane. His memory was a complete blank due to severe concussion; all he knew was that he was in Ireland with a blinding headache and double vision. The Japanese were most concerned about him. 'Forget about the Ulster,' they said, 'and try to get fit for the TT.'

Practising started the following week in the Isle of Man, over two months later than usual, the races having been delayed because of the seamen's strike. Bill travelled straight to the Island and tried to get plenty of rest.

Uncle Tom was so upset by Bill's accident that he redoubled his efforts to discover the cause of it. There was a definite fault somewhere in the bike, and it had to be found. The whole machine was dismantled and each part examined meticulously, but still nothing appeared to be wrong. Finally, in desperation, Tom sent the oil pipe to a research laboratory for analysis, but he was convinced there could be nothing wrong with it, for it was identical to that used on the bigger machine which had given no trouble whatsoever. However, the boffins came up with a startling discovery. By testing the pipe with oil running through it at the same pressure and temperature as on the machine, it swelled up like a balloon as the temperature increased, then it burst!

The pipe was of a special type which deteriorated over a period of time, even if it wasn't used, and should not have been used any longer than 12 months after manufacture. The pipe was found to be considerably older, yet Tom had purchased it from the AMC race department just before the season had started. When the factory was contacted they checked their invoices and found that almost their entire stock had been purchased in bulk, three years previously! The whole lot was a potential danger to anyone who used it, so it was destroyed, and warnings were issued in the Press urging all riders who had purchased an oil pipe from AMC to throw it away and replace it. The research laboratory discovered that the pipe Kirby had used on the 500cc machine had come from a completely different batch and was in good order. So the problem was solved, but poor Bill was the one who suffered. That wretched pipe could well have cost him a world title, for Taveri increased his championship lead by winning again in Ireland.

Ever since Bill had first visited the Isle of Man he had stayed at Mrs Lee's spotless little boarding house in Douglas. The homely atmosphere suited him far better than the hotels, and Mrs Lee was like a mother to him. She remembers vividly the first time Bill stayed with her:

'The first time I saw him was when this little chap came to my door and said, "Two of my friends are staying here – have you got room for me?" And his name was Ivy . . . goodness, he was only like a boy, and always funning with that "wicked" little look of his that endeared him to you – you couldn't help but love him really. I never saw him in any mood that wasn't good, and I never heard him say anything that you wouldn't have liked. He never went out of the door without turning back and giving you all the lip! The different things I used to say to him to try to get my own back, but he was always so quick-witted that he'd give you an answer back in a flash – and it would be better than yours!

'On his first stay here, when he came back from early morning practice, I said, "What do you want for breakfast?" He was a new fella to me, so I didn't know what he wanted. He said, "I'll have egg and chips and fried bread, please – and *I'll fry the bread!*" I said, "Oh, you will, will you?" Anyway, I did the egg and chips, and he got this piece of bread and put it under the cold water tap. He soaked it in water and dropped it in the fryer. I thought, "This fella's barmy!" And I said, "Well, Bill, what's *that* for?" "Well," he replied, "that's so the fat won't get in it!" I said, "Well, if *I* had fried it *I* wouldn't have let it get all fatty – I'm not *that* stupid!"

'One evening later in the week I was out in Douglas and I saw him strolling along the promenade hand-in-hand with my daughter, Jennifer! When he came in that night I pulled his leg and said, "I saw you tonight down on the prom'!" And he gave me that cheeky little look of his. "Mrs Lee," he said, "you've got a lovely daughter!"

'When he went out for practice one day he said, "I'm for the ambulance today!" And he did end up in it, too. He came back limping badly, but he only laughed. Even if he was in agony he was always laughing. I saw his back once when he had his shirt off. It was all carved up, and I thought, God . . . if that's racing!

'He liked the Island itself, but he didn't like the course. As far as he was concerned it was only a matter of work, and he was always glad when the racing was over. Despite this, the only time I ever saw him nervous was when he first went out for practice on the works Yamaha.'

When Ivy arrived at Mrs Lee's in 1966, he still felt far from well, but he never complained, and he made such an effort to be himself that nobody guessed just how bad he was. Although he rested as much as possible, he was still troubled by violent head-aches and bouts of blurred double vision. Some people might say that Ivy was a fool even to think of racing, but others would applaud his determination. The title of this chapter, 'service and courage', was Bill's old school motto, and it was a code by which he always tried to live. It wasn't the personal glory or the thought of winning the race for himself which spurred him on, he was think-ing of Yamaha's; he didn't want to let his team down. The Japanese had been good to him; they had given him his big break, they paid him well, and they accepted him, not only as a rider, but also as a friend. Ivy-San was conscious of his duty towards them, and he wasn't going to fail them, so he made up his mind that he was bloody well going to ride!

There was one drawback. The race officials would not allow Ivy to practice for the first two days, and then they insisted that he should produce a medical certificate stating that he was fit to ride before allowing him on the circuit. So Bill went to see one of the local doctors and casually asked to have his back examined. He explained that he needed a certificate passing him fit to race. The doctor looked at the ugly wound. 'Does it hurt?', he asked. 'Yes, a bit,' Bill replied, 'but it wouldn't affect my riding or impair my ability to control the bike.' The doctor seemed satisfied and scrib-bled out the vital document.

Walking out of the surgery with the certificate in his pocket, Ivy heaved a sigh of relief. They couldn't stop him riding now that he was pronounced fit. Of course, he hadn't mentioned anything to the doctor about being banged on the head – he'd just shown him his back. Luckily, the 'doc' was satisfied, but if he had given Ivy a thorough examination he would probably have ordered him straight to bed. He certainly wouldn't have passed him fit to race a motorcycle on the toughest course in the world!

Somehow Bill struggled through practice week, and in Sunday's 250cc event he put in a lap at over the magic 100 mph before retiring on the fourth lap whilst battling for second place. Through the speed trap his machine had recorded an almost unbelievable

150·6 mph, and only Hailwood and Agostini bettered this during the whole of race week, by just over 1 mph, when they were mounted on 500cc machines, twice the capacity of the Yamaha.

When Wednesday's 125cc race arrived, Bill felt a lot better, but he was still troubled by headaches and bad vision. This was the race that really mattered, and after the unpredictable Manx weather had delayed the start for almost three hours, the swirling mist which had enveloped the mountain, lifted, and the starting maroon went off to send the first pair of riders screaming away down Bray Hill. The battle was on, and Bill was determined to win. He needed those valuable points to keep him in the title chase, for if Taveri won he would clinch the championship for Honda.

In a nightmare ride Ivy staved off opposition from the Honda and Suzuki teams, as well as that of his team-mate Phil Read. But it was a frightening race, and here, in Bill's own words, is an account of what happened. (These details were not disclosed until several months after the race, in an interview with Mick Woollett of *Motor Cycle*.)

'I missed the first two days of practice, but finally they let me out on the Wednesday morning on a 125. I was getting headaches and could hardly see, but things improved. When I started in the race *I still must have been concussed*, otherwise I'd never have gone so fast. *It was sheer luck that I didn't crash!* On the first lap I'd just managed to catch and pass Taveri when I clouted the straw bales coming out of Schoolhouse Bend at Ramsey. Then I got on to the loose surface at the Gooseneck and clanged against an advertisement hoarding on the bank. Luigi went by as I was sorting myself out. He had a smile all over his face and that annoyed me. I caught him up again on the Mountain Mile.

'The second lap was a series of slides. The third was enjoyable. Things were back in focus again. No slides, no trouble, and just as fast – lovely.'

Bill Ivy had set the island alight with his incredible performance. He hoisted the race record up to 97·66 mph, and set a new lap record of 98·55 mph – 3 mph above the old record set up by Hugh Anderson the previous year. Phil Read finished second, with Anderson third, and in fourth place, after being out of racing for several months since his accident in Japan, was Mike Duff, back in the team again for just a couple of meetings.

By now Yamaha had brought out four-cylinder 125cc machines, but they were not used in the Island as their reliability had not been proved. However, the twins proved to be fast enough, and their consistency again clinched the manufacturers' team award. The Hondas of Mike Hailwood, Ralph Bryans, and championship leader Taveri, had all been out of tune. Apparently the carburation had been miscalculated, and the little five-cylinder machines sounded very off-song.

Yamahas were overjoyed, and so was Bill, for his win had put him back in the title chase. He began to feel more like his old self again, too, but he didn't realise just how lucky he had been until he saw a film of the race. Watching himself taking risks and bouncing off a wall frightened him to death. 'I *must* have been concussed,' he said, 'because I would *never* have ridden like that otherwise.'

Once again Ivy had achieved success, mainly through courage alone, but how many people would have gone through what he did to achieve victory? It is fortitude such as this that separates the super-men from the men; and Ivy came from the breed that enables a man to become a champion.

6

William the conqueror

THE OUTCOME of the 1966 125 cc world championship was decided in the Italian Grand Prix at Monza, where Luigi Taveri scored a fine victory. Although the five-cylinder Hondas were faster than the Yamahas they were often temperamental, but at Monza they were superb and there was nothing Ivy could do on such a fast circuit; he was relegated to third place by Taveri's team-mate, Ralph Bryans.

Naturally, Bill was disappointed about losing the championship, but to finish runner-up at his first attempt was a fine effort, and he rounded-off the season with a win in the Japanese Grand Prix. This pleased Yamaha's, for it was very satisfying to beat the rival Suzuki and Honda teams in their home classic.

Taveri, the brilliant and colourful little Swiss veteran, retired at the end of the year, and so did Hugh Anderson, the ex-champion from New Zealand. Honda withdrew from both 50 and 125 cc classes, and Yamaha's stiffest opposition during 1967 was to come from the Suzuki team of Stuart Graham (who had been dropped by Honda), Yoshimo Katayama, the Japanese rider, and the West German Hans George Anscheidt.

The 250 cc class developed into a straight fight between the Honda-sixes of Hailwood and Bryans, and the Yamaha-fours of Read and Ivy. Yamaha's team orders were for Ivy to try to win the 125 title, and for Read to be number-one in the bigger class.

When the season began Bill immediately went through another stage of knocking himself about. He fell off at speed at Brands Hatch while testing a 250 cc Yamaha and had to have his arm stitched, then he fell off again a week later while practising for the Spanish Grand Prix, this time hurting his leg. However, he made no mistakes in the race, and flung the nine-speed two stroke round at record speed to win comfortably, while Phil Read had the 250 cc race handed to him on a plate when Hailwood retired with a puncture after leading by a mile. Things had started off on the right foot for the Yamaha camp.

After this meeting Bill was featured in a *Motor Cycle News* inside column for which he wrote the following tongue-in-cheek article. It is of interest as another insight into his character, and because the article caused a certain amount of controversy:

'I am a bit battered and bruised – but dead chuffed mate! My ambition this year is to win a world championship and although I'm not going to stick my neck out with any predictions, winning the 125 class at the Spanish is as good a way to start the season as any.

'After crashing at about 120 mph while testing at Brands Hatch the other week – that was just about the luckiest escape I've ever had – and coming off during practice at Barcelona, I was not at all sure how the race would go.

'Another thing was that Phil Read and myself were told by Yamaha to ride the new four-cylinder 125s. We would rather have ridden the twins as they are easier to ride and handle better than the fours, but Yamaha thought otherwise. We argued, but that was it.

'As it happened everything turned out all right, though my bike went on to three cylinders towards the end of the race. I was a worried man for those last five laps. The problem with the fours is that they tend to oil-up the plugs on slow corners, and on the Montjuich Park circuit there aren't enough straight bits to clear them again.

'It should be better this weekend for the West German GP at Hockenheim – plenty of long straights. Boy do I like straights, you can keep your corners.

After the race in Spain we had a bit of a booze-up. There was Mike Hailwood, Phil Read and a few of us other lads. We were staying on a camping site just outside Barcelona on the shores of the Med'.

'There is always plenty of leg-pulling at these parties and poor old Mike came in for his fair share about his flat tyre in the 250 race.

'A few drinks help you to relax after the race but I don't touch the stuff during practice or before a race. This year my whole purpose is to win a world championship. I still go out with the dollies and when I have a ball I really have a ball, but racing comes first.

'After I fell off at Brands I got well slewed because I was so happy that I could crash at 120 mph and still be healthy enough to go out in the evening. The Yamaha – it was one of those 250 twins they built specially for us – was written off. It seized as I was going over the top of the brow into Paddock Bend. I think I must have been asleep because I knew about it ages before I started to do anything about it. So now I only have a 125 twin for private use, but I am hoping to do a few races with it later in the season.

'I have been lucky as far as racing is concerned, but my car was not so lucky in Barcelona. Some thieves broke into it and stole my typewriter, and then the clutch pedal broke off. The Ossa factory kindly welded it back on for me. The car is an American Stingray which I bought last year from Luigi Taveri. It is a great crumpet-wagon and I like 'gi-normous' engines. I think I will have another one this year, but with a 7 litre motor. I wouldn't mind an Iso Grifo like Mike Hailwood's but they are so common these days – must be at least a dozen in the country! It is essential to have something which motors a bit because we do a lot of miles between races on the Continent. Mike and I often cruise at about 130 mph on the autobahns.

'Being a works rider and doing all the world championship meetings is very different from racing at home. I won't say I like it better, but it's certainly different. We are always testing and sorting-out troubles, especially on the new machines. Everything is different and has to be sorted-out. When you come in during practice you have to be able to explain to the mechanics exactly what is happening. Not like the old Nortons and Ajays – they were sorted 50 years ago! I am concentrating on motorbike racing now and I intend riding Yamahas as long as they want me. Car racing is out because I know that you cannot successfully mix the two. And I like bike racing – especially when I'm right out in front!'

Bill's article caused quite a few people to take umbrage, even though it was written in a humorous vein. One young lady was so incensed that she wrote to MCN the following week and condemned the inside column with Bill Ivy as 'quite nauseating', and went on to say: 'We would like to know the behind-the-scenes activities of professional motorcyclists with racing and bikes – NOT their sex life. If we want to read this sort of thing we can read 'Playboy'. And really, does Bill Ivy have to be so nasty about Nortons and Ajays being sorted-out 50 years ago? There was no need for this – at least they're British.'

This letter, written by a Miss Pauline Hallybone from London, spurred Bill into grabbing for his pen again and writing a letter to defend himself which was published in the next issue of MCN. He apologised for upsetting anyone and said that his comments were not intended to be taken too seriously, adding: 'Even the most fanatical enthusiast has to leave motorbikes alone sometimes. What do people expect us to do between race meetings on the Continent – sit and read?' He went on to say that he didn't mean to be rude about British bikes, but they had been designed a long time ago, and IF there was a British machine capable of winning a world championship he would like to ride it. Bill concluded by saying, 'But I am not ashamed of riding for a foreign team. Yamaha is a good team to ride for and they spend a lot of money on racing, so they deserve to be successful.'

For a person who is constantly in the public eye it is often easy to become out of favour with some people. This was especially so in Ivy's case, for his sense of humour was sometimes misunderstood, but the majority of his fans loved his outrageous pranks and witty remarks. Most professional motorcyclists are reserved and shun away from the limelight. Their performances on the track receive the spectators' interest and appreciation, but once out of the saddle they create no more than a casual interest because they are not colourful characters. The three notable exceptions were Hailwood, Agostini and Ivy. Apart from being super-stars on two wheels they had 'film star' images. Wherever they went and whatever they did, whether at the race tracks or out on the town, they always attracted the attention of the general public. People would crowd round in the paddocks, jostling and shoving for a glimpse of them. There was a never-ending stream of autograph-hunters, and the gorgeous dollies were always flocking round – that was the bit Bill enjoyed most of all. These three were the principal characters in the whole scene, and they received the acclaim of fans the world over. As Cassius Clay was to boxing, and George Best to football, so were these the star attractions of motorcycling, the men the crowds really came to see.

Hailwood and Ivy were nearly always together, typifying the comradeship which exists between the majority of the two-wheeled racing fraternity. They were rivals committed to different companies, and would ride hell for leather against each other on the track, yet they were the best of friends. They would chase after the girls together, race from one country to another in their cars, and have a whale of a time socially. Then, when it came down to busi-

Right: Another garland, a smile and a wave, this time for a victory at Cadwell Park on the 125cc Yamaha. *Below:* On the way to the chequered flag Bill aviates the Yamaha up 'The Mountain'.

Above: Two masters in action. Bill Ivy (250cc Yamaha) leads Mike Hailwood (250cc Honda) at Mosport Park during the 1967 Canadian Grand Prix. *Left:* Two 'hippies' in action. In very different gear, Bill and Mike demonstrate a spot of flower power in the paddock at Snetterton!

The four-cylinder Yamaha – a masterpiece
of sophisticated engineering.

First signs of 'the needle'? More than the usual amount of pre-race tension seems evident on the faces of Bill Ivy and Phil Read as they line-up for the start of the 125cc TT race in 1968.

Above left: Bill with Phil Read at Sachsenring, East Germany, in 1968. *Left:* Bill regains the track at Monza after the excursion which cost him the 250cc title. *Above:* Ivy leads during the 1968 250cc Dutch GP. *Right:* This time Read is inches ahead as the Yamaha men duel in the rain at Imatra on their 250s; nine laps later Ivy fell at this corner in pursuit of Read.

Left: Occasional outbursts against officialdom exposed the tension which existed beneath Bill's usually jovial manner ... *Below:* But he was invariably on the best of terms with his ever-smiling Japanese mechanics, especially after he had won!

ness and the flag dropped, they were out to win – that's what they were paid to do. Possibly because of their friendship the rivalry between them was particularly intense, but once the races were over, whoever won, there was never any bitterness between them over success and defeat. Both were sportsmen and neither went in for excuses, although they would laugh and pull each other's legs unmercifully.

This spirit of competition was extended beyond the race tracks when they embarked on the long journeys from one venue to the next in their cars. 'We had quite a few burn-ups,' Mike recalls. 'We had a fantastic dice from Zurich to Clermont-Ferrand once. Bill was in his Stingray and I had a Ferrari. We diced it up all the way, and the cars were smoking, steaming wrecks by the time we got there – we did it in some fantastic time. And there was another one from Barcelona to somewhere . . . that was a bit hectic, too!

'Then there was that business in the Island. . .!' The recollection of this was accompanied by the infectious Hailwood grin. 'There was a bird working in the Hawaiian Bar, and she wanted to go for a ride in Bill's new Ferrari. So we all leapt aboard with her in the middle and went charging off down past 'The Highlander' on the TT course at about 140 mph. As we came up to Greeba Castle, I said, "Bill, you're going a bit too fast – you're never going to get round." And he said, "Oh, we'll be all right, we'll get through." We got round the first bit but arrived at the next corner in a great big broadside, and he over-corrected it and went into the wall. We went along the wall for about 50 yards and tore the side out of the bloody car – and this bird was having kittens! It was quite frightening.'

Mrs Lee remembers when Bill came back to his lodgings after the accident: 'He came creeping in, and I knew he'd smashed his lovely new car up because a policeman had brought one of the wheels here – it was all buckled up. Bill told me what had happened and said that they had a dollie-bird with them, and afterwards she'd been leaning over the wall "peukin" with shock. "I don't wonder at it," I told him, "it's a wonder you're all still alive." I said, "It's a good job you never killed the other fella, because by God his old man would have been up here and you'd have been for the high jump!"'

Of course, all the newspapers got hold of the story and Bill had a job to live it down – all the boys ribbed him about it. He told the police that he got a flat tyre going into the corner, and although they couldn't prove otherwise Bill was still fined £12 for dangerous

F

driving. It proved to be a very expensive affair, for the wall had to be paid for, and worst of all, as the car had been purchased in Italy it was only on comprehensive insurance cover whilst in that country – everywhere else it was only on third party. Bill did his nut when he discovered this, for he had to pay for the repairs himself, which amounted to £1,000! On top of that, he'd only had the car for a month!

Before he bought the Ferrari Bill had to use his wits to extract himself from an awkward situation while driving the Stingray back from London one night. He always called the Stingray 'The Pudding' because he considered it handled badly. 'It's a nice car,' he used to say, 'but it's sloppy on corners – like a bloody pudding!' Whether it handled badly or not, Ivy would put it through a corner at a speed which would have had most people grabbing for the toilet roll. On this particular night he was driving at his usual pace, the road was deserted, and the police saw him tramping through a built-up area. They gave chase, but hadn't a snowball in hell's chance of catching him, so they radioed HQ and a road block was set-up farther down the road. Bill had no alternative but to stop. He knew he was for the high jump because he'd been doing colossal speeds through the 30 mph limits. As he screeched to a halt and wound the window down Ivy's quick brain was working overtime. A policeman walked over to the car.

'Do you know what speed you were doing?'

'Eh?'

The question was repeated.

'No spleak English!'

The policeman was temporarily taken aback then he began to speak slowly and very deliberately in an effort to make himself understood. To no avail, for the little 'foreigner' just sat in his 'pudding' (which fortunately had Swiss registration plates), and looked vacant. Every now and then he burst into a completely unintelligible stream of gibberish, which he invented on the spur of the moment. In exasperation, the policeman called out to his mates.

'Here, any of you lot speak German – we've got a bloomin' Kraut here!' And they all had a try at making themselves understood. Ivy had the cheek of the devil. He was actually enjoying himself, and it was all he could do to stop himself from giving the game away by bursting out laughing. Eventually one of the policemen had the right idea. He pointed to the speedometer and made signs.

'Ah, ah ... KILOMETER?!' Bill ventured enthusiastically.

The police were convinced that they had a hopeless case, but they seemed satisfied that the little 'foreign bloke' ('He's not German – I don't know what he is') understood what he had done wrong. They gesticulated that he could go, smiled and bade goodnight as the car poodled gently off into the night, its occupant waving excitedly and bidding goodbye in 'double-Dutch'.

Few people would have the nerve to pull-off such a trick, but if they did they would probably congratulate themselves and consider that it would be tempting providence ever to attempt anything remotely like it again, even though it would take pride of place among their pub stories, and be related over a pint for many years. But to Ivy it was the perfect alibi, and one that he used many times, especially when parking in London. He would think nothing of leaving his car in the middle of the West End, half on the road and half on the pavement, straddling double yellow lines. He would amble off to the shops and return with an 'innocent air' to confront the traffic warden pacing round his car, but never once was he booked . . . the foreigner act never failed.

Having learned all the grand prix circuits and how to handle the tricky Yamahas the previous year, Ivy was obviously in a much stronger position during 1967. After starting the season so well with his win in the Spanish GP he was favourite to win the class in West Germany, but this event was a disaster for both the Yamaha men.

Despite being virtually last away Ivy took the lead after six laps, and Read was right with him as they closed up on two riders who were being lapped. Then one of them fell half-way round a bend, bringing the other down with him, right in the path of the screaming Yamahas. Bill almost got through, but one of the fallen machines struck him and down he went, and poor Phil sailed into the lot and was catapulted head-first into the bank. The incident would have deterred some of the hardest riders, but Ivy and Read licked their wounds and lined-up for the following 250 event.

Phil was robbed of victory in the race after Hailwood retired; after stopping for a plug change he tore through the field to finish second, cutting leader Ralph Bryans' 40-seconds advantage to a mere 4 by the end of the race. Bill established a new absolute lap record of 111·49 mph for the Hockenheim circuit before retiring with gearbox trouble.

Shortly afterwards Bill collapsed in Mike Hailwood's caravan and was whisked off to hospital suffering from delayed shock. It was the sixth time he had crashed since the beginning of the season but the first time he had fallen in a race – all the other prangs had been during practice. The doctors advised Bill to rest for a few days, and by the time the French GP arrived he was not only fit, but in tremendous form. He won the 125cc event, smashing both lap and race records, then went on to win the 250 race as well, scoring his first classic double.

The 250 was a very strange race, for Ivy, Read and Hailwood all took turns to lead, only to drop back, one by one, as they hit trouble. Bill was on the point of pulling in with gearbox trouble, but then Mike's gearbox started playing up, and Phil's clutch cable broke, making it difficult for him to select his gears. The lead changed several times, with each rider trying to coax his ailing machine home first. Bill eventually won from Phil, with Mike third, but he wasn't happy about the way he had won it and apologised to Hailwood afterwards!

It was a different tale in the 250 TT, for only two seconds covered the trio after the first lap, and they were all travelling at record-breaking pace; Mike was in his usual position with Phil second and Bill third. There was still very little between them at the end of the second lap, and all were averaging over 103 mph. Then the maestro increased his lead relentlessly, Phil pulled away from Bill, and the pattern seemed set, until Bill's Yamaha broke its crankshaft.

In Hailwood's opinion, Ivy was never quite as good on the 250 as he was on the 125, not because he lacked anything in ability, or because of his size, but mainly because of his lack of weight. On bumpy sections, especially in the Island, Bill really found the 250 a handful. On a fast, smooth circuit being light didn't matter, but in the Isle of Man some sections are so rough it's like riding over a ploughed field at 100 mph, and he had to hang on for grim death. He once told his mother that riding the 250 over there was like sitting on a 'bucking bronco'. And it was the one place where he didn't want her to watch him. 'I don't want you worrying about me over there, Ethel,' Bill told her. 'It would really frighten you – it frightens *me* . . . scares the bloody pants off me it does!'

Despite this handicap, Bill gave Mike a hard time on several occasions in 1967, the last year 'Ace' contested the world championships before switching to motor racing. 'We were often at it, and I remember that particular race in the Island. I started 10 seconds in front of Bill, and coming over the Mountain on the first lap I could look back and see him. He must have been really flying, but I think he frightened himself so much that he slowed down a bit. Yes, we had a lot of dices that year.

'Really, Bill was as good as anybody, but I think he was rather handicapped by his lack of weight on the bigger bikes. I'm not saying that he wasn't strong, because he was tremendously strong and fit, but he was just a bit too light.

'On the 125's he was better than anybody. Probably, on his day, Luigi Taveri was as good as Bill, and possibly Phil Read was about the same when he really got his finger out. Bill's determination was a fantastic thing.

'I remember the first time he went ski-ing in Switzerland. We were staying with Luigi. Bill had never been ski-ing before, and although it looks easy, it's not – it's very difficult. He had a try up and down by the house, and said, "Ah, that's easy isn't it? I'm coming up to the ski-lift with you, Luigi!" And Luigi said, "No, no, you must have some lessons first." Bill said, "No, that's all right, it looks easy enough – I can do it." Luigi wasn't at all happy about it, but Bill insisted, so they went right to the top of the ski-lift, and it's a long way up. They set off early one afternoon and old Bill fell over in the region of 90 *times*! He was so determined to master it that he wouldn't give up. They kept going on and on and eventually got back when it was dark – but he got back in the end. Considering the time he spent at it (which wasn't much), he could ski quite well in the finish.'

The TT celebrated its Diamond Jubilee that year, but there was nothing for Ivy to celebrate, for he retired again in the 125 event when the gremlins struck on the second lap. All Bill had to show for his visit to the Island was a bent and very second-hand-looking Ferrari, but although success eluded him he was still as popular as ever.

One afternoon Mrs Lee was busy in her boarding house when there was a knock at the door. 'I went to see who it was,' she recalls, 'and there was this little boy standing there. He showed me a photo, and the rider was nearly off the picture. He said, "That's Bill – that's *Bill Ivy*!" I said, "Oh aye, but why didn't you get him in the middle?" He said, "Well, I thought I had him, I thought I had him . . . if I leave it here do you think he'll put his autograph on it?" I said, "Well, come in at tea time and ask him."

'He came back later and gave the picture to Bill. "It's YOU!", he said. Bill said, "Yes, I know it's me but what am I doing over here?" (pointing to the tiny unidentifiable dot in the extreme corner of the photo). "Well," the little boy said, "I thought I had you – *but you went too fast!*" He was so proud, that little fella. . . . his mother said that he got so excited about seeing Bill that later he got a high temperature. He was only about seven years old, and he'd got a picture of Bill Ivy, even though it was just a dot on a film!'

Onwards from the TT to the Dutch TT, where Ivy scored two second places, behind Read in the 125 and Hailwood in the 250. Then he won the smaller class in East Germany and finished second to Read in the 250. Ivy was superb on the 125, and race and lap records tumbled as he established his superiority in the class with a hat-trick of wins in Czechoslovakia, the Ulster GP, and the Italian round at Monza where finally he clinched the world championship. William had conquered!

With only two rounds remaining in the 250 title chase, Ivy also stood a chance of taking this as well, for only six points covered Read, himself, Bryans and Hailwood, in that order. But Phil Read was the man Yamahas really wanted to win this class, so Bill had to back-up his team-mate.

At the Canadian GP Mike Hailwood won from Phil Read, but Bill failed to add to his score because his bike went sick and he had to retire. Everything now hinged on the final round in Japan – or did it? As it turned out, none of the championship contenders finished the race. Mike went out first of all, with ignition trouble. Then Phil joined him with a broken crankshaft, leaving Hiroshi Hasegawa and Bill out in front. Then Hasegawa's Yamaha broke its crank, and a few laps later Bill's did the same. Ralph Bryans eventually won, but he hadn't enough points to take the title. As it turned out, Mike Hailwood, who had had a shocking run of bad luck throughout the year, retained his title for Honda, but it had been a very close thing. He and Read tied on points, but as Mike had five wins to Phil's four the honour went to him, and Bill finished third, a mere four points behind. It ended in rather an anti-climax after a struggle which had been tremendously close throughout the season.

Bill didn't mind about failing to win the 250 title, for after all he had achieved his ultimate ambition of winning a world championship, and in only his second classic season. It didn't pay to be too greedy, so he was quite satisfied with the 125 championship hoping that there would be a chance of having a go at the double some time in the future.

7

Just William and the image

MANY PEOPLE THOUGHT that Bill Ivy changed when he became famous, and to a certain extent he did, but only superficially. As he became more successful, so he became more flamboyant. After winning the world championship he grew his hair long, and took to wearing trendy clothes long before the new mode of fashion really caught on. He was the first motorcycling personality to portray the style which developed into the trend of the Seventies. This was in 1967–8, when our so-called 'respectable' society viewed the changing scene with an air of disgust, and fashion-conscious young men with long hair were frowned upon by the short-back-and-sides brigade. Quite a lot of narrow-minded people couldn't see past Ivy's long locks and showy manner, but they were the type of people who couldn't see past a lot of things that weren't conventional.

Even Mrs Ivy tried to talk Bill into getting his hair cut, because she was worried about what people might think, and eventually Bill gave in and paid a visit to the barber's. 'I've had it cut, Ethel,' he said on his return. He had, too – half an inch all over! After that his mother gave up trying!

Ivy offended nobody and nothing except convention, and although some people condemned him for it, the image which he created in public endeared him to countless thousands of fans. The big Ferrari or Maserati, parked willy-nilly in the paddock with the stereo tape recorder blaring out pop music; the 'with it', long-haired little character, ambling nonchalantly down to the pits with a cute dollie on each arm and a huge grin in between; the glamour, the laughter, the fun, the occasional brush with officialdom, the outrageous pranks . . . this was Bill Ivy in public, until he wriggled into his skin-tight leathers, donned his silver crash helmet with the green ivy leaf emblem on the front, and straddled one of the 150 mph Yamaha projectiles. Then was the image cast aside, for it was no longer necessary; the entertainer was still entertaining, but with his skill and daring. On the circuit or off it, the public can never say that Ivy gave them anything less than their money'sworth.

In 1967, at an International meeting at Snetterton, the organisers were rather amused when two hippies walked into the race office and said that they had come to sign-in as they were competing. The officials, thinking that the way-out pair had probably found their way into the paddock the night before without paying, decided to go along with the joke. 'Right – what numbers are you?', they asked. The tall, Indian-looking fellow answered, 'Number one.' This seemed to amuse the grinning officials even more. 'No,' they said, 'you can't be number one – Mike Hailwood's number one!' The game went on for quite some time, then the organisers realised that the joke was on them, for the two 'hippies' were none other than Mike and Bill, heavily disguised with wigs and all the gear!

On another occasion, Bill was the guest of honour at an official function which was being held in a plush hotel. After dinner the floor was cleared for dancing, but Bill, usually the centre of such activities, was nowhere to be seen. It was a hot evening, and he had discovered that the hotel had a swimming pool. So he stripped down to his underwear and jumped in for a quick dip. Somebody found out where he was, and it wasn't long before others followed suit. In the end there were more people swimming than there were dancing, and even some of the girls went in, clad in bras and panties.

Socially, Ivy was completely unpredictable, especially at the after-meeting functions when even some of the most reserved riders let their hair down as part of the unwinding ritual. Bill was in great form at the Dutch TT prizegiving one year and he frightened and astonished everybody by standing on his hands, on two beer glasses, perched on top of a table laden with drinks – if he had lost his balance and fallen he would have been cut to ribbons.

Through living dangerously, racing drivers and motorcyclists also tend to enjoy life more intensely. They gamble their lives, and frightening incidents are all part and parcel of their existence, which they accept. Frequently one hears that top racing men 'have no nerves', but this is rubbish. They experience the same feelings, fears and emotions as anyone else, and if you ask any of them if they have ever been really frightened, most will be honest enough to admit that they have. The difference between them and other people is that they are strong-willed and push these feelings to one side. They have the ability to control them, which enables them to reach higher and more exacting standards without panicking. With a cool head and lightning-fast reactions, they can tackle hazards at speeds which lesser mortals would never attempt. To them, success is the reward – everything else is of secondary importance. They are always aware of the danger, but the fear of it is pushed into the subconscious.

Then, when it is all over, they want an outlet. All the pent-up nervous energy is released, and replaced by an overwhelming desire to have a rave-up. To those who have been lucky enough to win, success can be very intoxicating. They fidget, bubble over with exuberance, and look for something – anything – on which to expend their feelings. A lot of riders feel the need to unwind after the day's battles, and some of the Continental get-togethers are riotous affairs. Although the majority of the motorcycle boys are reserved in public, amongst their own crowd they really let their hair down like a coachload of kids on an outing.

As far as Mike and Bill were concerned, they didn't really care where they were or, within reason, what they did. If they felt like a wild spree they would have one, and the section of society which knows and understands nothing about racing or the men who race, has frequently had cause to raise its eyebrows in amazement at the antics of Messrs Hailwood and Ivy. Indeed, the residents of the luxury block of flats where Mike and Bill lived could have been forgiven for wondering on occasions whether motorcycle racers were entirely normal.

One Sunday morning around 6 a.m. William decided to clear-up his flat after one of their parties, but instead of emptying all the rubbish down the waste chute in one go, he decided to emulate the actions of a wartime naval officer by 'depth-charging' an imaginary submarine with the empty beer cans one at a time. . . .

'Fire one!' Clatter – clatter – clatter. 'Fire two!' Clatter – clatter – clatter. So it went on as Captain William David Ivy (slightly intoxicated) plotted the downfall of the enemy submarine from the bridge of his destroyer, and from the seemingly inexhaustible supply of depth charges, finally succeeded in scoring a direct hit with the very last one. Captain William then tottered off to his bunk, happy in the knowledge that he alone had saved the allies from defeat, as his long-suffering neighbours emerged from under their pillows, rolled over, cursed the idiot upstairs for the hundredth time, and tried to get back to sleep.

These parties were a huge success among the racing fraternity, and there was rarely a shortage of girls. But if there was, Bill would jump in his car and tour up and down the Kings Road, chatting-up any dollies who happened to be around and asking them if they wanted to go to a party. He always ended up with a carload!

But while Ivy was fun-loving and at times mischievous, rather like an overgrown schoolboy, what of the real Billy beneath that exterior? In many ways he was vastly different from the image which surrounded him, and at times public façade completely belied the true character of the man. As a result, although many acquaintances thought they knew him, few people really did know or understand him.

There are two distinct schools of thought regarding Ivy's flamboyance. Some say that he was a natural showman who loved to entertain, and others are of the opinion that because he lived in company with Mike Hailwood (a natural extrovert), he felt that he ought to have 'an act'. Certainly, he was a home-loving boy who had led a comparatively sheltered existence, and then had found himself pitched into a rather artificial life by virtue of his outstanding success at racing. At first he had felt out of his depth, socially, and possibly because of this he adopted a personality which he considered appropriate once he had gained the limelight – but overdid it somewhat. Then, because he earned the reputation of being an extrovert, the public *expected* him to be unconventional and the situation overtook him, so he played along with it. Whatever the reason, Bill was different in a crowd to the Bill with just a few close friends around him.

Ron Eldridge, who acted as Bill's mechanic in 1968, recalls:

'Bill was different in the paddock or among a crowd; then he was the life and soul of the party, and really he just had to show-off. For example, he wouldn't put his leathers on by himself at the side of the van – he'd stand in the middle of the paddock and get everybody to help him! One day, he wanted to rub some preserving oil into his leathers, but he didn't lay them out in the back of the van and do them himself like most people would. He put on his leathers, stood in the middle of the paddock and got two or three of the 'village idiots' to perform the task as a whole crowd gathered round to watch the performance. He was definitely a showman!'

In view of some of his exploits, it may come as a surprise to some people to learn that Ivy was very vulnerable. 'He was extremely sensitive for a man,' said Sue Ivy. 'It was very easy to hurt his feelings over some things.'

Harry Downing, the BP Competitions Manager, was surprised

to discover this, and he had known Bill for a long time. 'I can't remember the exact circumstances,' said Harry, 'but it was something to do with one of the riders being killed or seriously injured. At the time I was discussing it with Bill, and he was almost in tears. He was really upset about it, and I hadn't realised that he was such a sensitive, emotionally vulnerable person until then.

'The thing was, you had to get to know little Bill. When I really got to know him the thing that really impressed me was the way that he looked after his mother. Even when he got to the top of the tree he never forgot her. There aren't many lads who would have regarded their mothers with so much affection at his age. To look at Bill, with his trendy clothes and long hair, you wouldn't have realised that a bloke like that could be so human and think about his mother in the way that he did – and I think this was great.

'Shortly after he became a works rider I was talking to him at one meeting when two other riders came up and started asking questions about certain lines on the circuit. These two lads were only novices and were obviously struggling and doing it the hard way. Now a lot of top riders (and I could name them) can't be bothered to take much trouble in helping anyone, but Bill offered to take them out on to the circuit to show them the way round. He said, "If you'd like to follow me round for a few laps, I'll show you the lines I take – and I hope they're the correct lines!" To me, that was more than fantastic. To take this trouble with two novices was fabulous.

'He was marvellous about meeting his public, too. Bill was never too aloof to look after those who idolised him. He was never too busy to sign autographs, irrespective of how hectic things had been – or even if he had lost.'

Ivy's confident air, his remarks, and his showy manner were often misinterpreted. If some people saw him larking about in front of a crowd, they immediately thought, 'Look at the little show-off . . . who does he think he is?', and assume wrongly that Bill was a big-head. Frank Higley has something to say about this:

'I've heard people say that Bill was big-headed, and this was bad because it was very untrue – I think he would sooner have crawled away in the back of the van and forgotten about the whole thing. To me he was a gentleman, a true champion, and a rider who would always give that little bit extra. When he stopped riding for me and went on to Yamaha, whenever he saw me he always spoke, and was always appreciative for what I'd done for him. If he saw me at a race meeting he would always come up and want to start a conversation. He would never pass by and pretend that he hadn't seen you. I've had riders who have been just the opposite and didn't want to know you any more once they'd moved on.

'We had great fun together – never any problems or rows. To me he was a chap that you just couldn't row with, although people say that if he had a difference of opinion he would argue to the ends of the earth; I never had a difference of opinion with him. Some riders are always dissatisfied, and you can never do enough for them, but Bill was always the other way round. He was one of the easiest riders to get on with that I've ever sponsored, which is a lot to say. With the majority of riders I've had, if something goes wrong, they either want to kick the bike or throw it down and get into a panic, but Bill never did this at all.

'I think he was very much a professional. He was in it for gain, but he was also in it for pleasure. He was a chap that liked success, definitely, but if he was beaten fair and square he would admit defeat in a sportsmanlike manner, which was a great thing. And Bill was a *dedicated* rider, which is something that I find lacking today. Nowadays, so many riders seem to be in it just for the glory and the good times.'

One day, Bill overheard somebody saying that he was bigheaded, so he went over to the person and tried to explain how he felt. He said that it was very difficult to know quite what to do in his position, even with regards to passing the time of day. 'If I say "Hello" and start talking to some people, I often get the impression that they're thinking "Who the hell does he think he is . . . barging in and interrupting!" On the other hand, if people are engrossed in conversation and I pass by, afterwards I think that perhaps I should have spoken, and I wonder if they had noticed me and said "Oh, he's out of our class now – doesn't want to know us – bloody snob."' He said that he didn't want people thinking that he was pushing himself on them because he was Bill Ivy, but he was frightened of ignoring them in case they thought he was snobbish. Consequently, he was never quite sure what to do.

Ron Eldridge said: 'I think Bill's biggest problem was that he wanted to please everybody. He was very sensitive about what people thought of him, and he could be very easily hurt by things that were said about him.'

No, Ivy certainly wasn't swollen-headed, conceited or otherwise affected by his success. Although he appeared a shade cocky, he was really extremely modest. He enjoyed the hero-worship and the fuss that was made of him in the spheres of his racing life, but he never pushed himself, advertised the fact that he was a champion, or even raised the topic of motorcycling among people whom he met who had no knowledge or interest in the sport. He would get furious with his father for introducing him to people by saying, 'This is my son . . . you know who he is, don't you?' Naturally, Ringo was very proud of Bill, and he wanted to let people know that his son was famous, but Bill would get very ratty about it. 'Dad,' he would say, 'I'm no different to any other sportsman, and it's everyone to their own sport. It would be the same as asking me who the top cricketers are – I wouldn't have a clue. If somebody introduced me to one and said, "You know who this is, don't you?", I'd be most embarrassed having to say, "No, I'm sorry but I don't – who is it?"'

Mrs Ivy often had girls phoning up and asking for Bill, and when she told them he was abroad, as frequently he was, they would ask if he was on holiday. 'No,' she would tell them, 'he's away racing.' Bill had never told them that he was a professional racing motorcyclist. 'Why should I tell them?', he said to his mother. 'I tell them my name, and if they don't know anything about racing then they obviously wouldn't have heard of me. They're friendly with me because I'm Bill Ivy – not Bill Ivy the motorcyclist!'

Bill always considered himself as one of the lucky ones, because he had always been sponsored in racing. He appreciated the fact that he'd never had to struggle financially as do most riders. He said that a lot of riders would have made it to the top if they'd had the same chances as he'd had, but instead, they had to pack up because they couldn't afford competitive machinery.

Another thing about him was that he was very sincere and kind-hearted. He would put himself out to help anyone, even if he didn't know them. For example, Bill received a letter one day from a man whose teenage son was in hospital through a motorcycle accident. The boy's leg had been amputated, and he was feeling very low. Apparently he idolised Bill, so his father wrote and asked for an autographed photo, which he felt would cheer the lad up. That same afternoon Bill drove down to the coast, picked up the boy's father, and together they went to the hospital. The patient was thrilled to pieces, and so was his dad, in more ways than one as apparently Bill's driving scared him stiff! But it goes without saying how much this act of kindness was appreciated.

Very few people maintain connections with their school after they leave, but this was another thing about Bill which was completely out of character with his accepted public image. Mr Cocksedge, Ivy's old woodwork master, explains:

'We didn't see much of Bill for a while once he left Chisholm's, but we heard how well he was doing at his racing. Then one day a great big car pulled up and parked right in front of the school. Everybody was asking whose it was, then who should walk round the back but young William. From then on he used to pop in periodically during the Winter, and by this time we were on Christian-name terms. "Whato Bob," he used to say, but he never used my Christian name in the classroom in front of the children – it was always "Mr Cocksedge". Directly we got into the staffroom it was "Bob", the curtain dropped down and there he was, just little Bill again.

'I used to ask him how he was getting on, and he would recount all his adventures. He was always genuinely honest, and he'd tell the truth about things. I remember him telling us once that he would never be as good as Mike Hailwood, and he told us one day that he knew the risks he was taking. "Oh well," he said, "I know it's dangerous – it's a short life! I'll try to make my fortune and then retire." He admitted that he had been really scared at times. "Really scared?" I asked. "*Bloody* scared," he said. It takes guts to admit that, so you couldn't say that he was a big-headed boy, and when he came back to the school he had every opportunity of being so.

'To roll up in a car that was equivalent to . . . say, *twice* the headmaster's annual salary, for one thing. I mean, he could have come to the school and been thoroughly objectionable, but this was one of Billy's many good points; he never let on how good he was – you literally had to drag it out of him. And he always respected the teachers. He often used to stay to lunch with us in the staffroom, and he could have bragged like blazes, but he would never push himself forward.

'During the Winter he used to get a bit out of condition, so he would come down to the school and train with the boys in the gym two or three afternoons a week. He was also busy trying to get off with the domestic science teacher! Bill almost had the run of the place because he was a celebrity down at the school. All the kids idolised him and he always had a crowd round him – he was very popular.

'He took me out for a little spin in his Ferrari when he first bought it – scared me to death!

'I think he did put on a flamboyant act in front of some people, but when one really knew him, as we knew him, I couldn't have wished to meet a nicer chap. When he first began to grow his hair long I said, in fun, "It's about time you had it cut!" He just grinned. "Oh, this is the style now," he said.

'He wanted to do something for the school, but he said that he would like to do something especially for the "thick-'uns" as he called them. He'd always considered himself as a "thick-'un", and he wanted to donate an award to give the less able ones a chance of winning a trophy. Bill donated £25, and we had these fountain pens made with "Bill Ivy" inscribed on them. Each term we present one to the most deserving boy – not necessarily the brainiest boy, but the one who has made the effort and really tried. We made a small trophy out of stainless steel, of a racing motorcyclist at speed, and the boy who wins the award keeps this for a term and takes it home to show his parents.

'When Bill presented the trophy for the first time he gave us a speech, and it was the nicest little speech I think I've ever heard. The actual content of it was modest. He didn't appeal to the brainy ones of the school, he just told the "thick-'uns" (that was the exact term he used) how much they owed the school, how much it was doing for them, and how much it had done for him. He had a genuine affection for Old Borough Manor as he knew it, and this is something that I really admired him for. The impression I have of Bill, was that he was a very nice lad, a very nice young man, and a gentleman to boot.'

With some professional riders, once they get to the top all they think about is making a pile of money. They don't seem to enjoy the sport any longer, and only remain in it for what they can get out of it. This was not so in Ivy's case, for his enthusiasm and love of the sport was such that it was not uncommon to find him down at Brands Hatch spectating at novice meetings. He would sit on the barrier at Paddock Bend for the greater part of the afternoon, taking a keen interest in what was going on, and he was only too willing to give his advice to anyone who asked.

On one such afternoon he spotted a young lad on a battered old bike running rings round other riders with far more expensive up-to-date machinery. He wasn't winning, but he caught Bill's eye with his obvious style and natural ability, so much so that Bill contacted Uncle Tom and a trial was arranged for the promising youngster. The result was encouraging, and the lad was given a regular place in the Kirby team. This was Pat Mahoney's big break, and he went on to become a star and win a British Championship, but if it hadn't have been for Bill . . . who knows?

Roy Francis had kept up his racing, too, and although his successes could in no way be compared to Bill's, he had done quite well. Even though he was away on the Continent most of the time, Bill always kept track of how Roy had been doing in England through the motorcycling Press. He would make a mental note of Roy's achievements, and when he next saw his friend he never failed to comment on them. They say that it's the little things in life that mean a lot, and those little comments meant a hell of a lot to Roy.

Bill had very few really close friends, but if he befriended someone he never forgot them, and he was very loyal in every respect except one. Mike Hailwood explains.

'He was a very loyal friend except for one thing – and that was when it came to birds. *He used to pinch mine!* We used to do a bit of mutual pinching, I suppose, but when he first moved into the flat he didn't know as many girls as I did, so he used to chase after mine!

'But he was very loyal, and very kind. Whenever I had trouble with my car, if I was working on it, or fiddling around with a bike or something, he'd say, "Go on – get out of the bloody way and I'll do it for you", because he used to see me making a hack of it. Even if he had work of his own to do, he'd get stuck in and do mine and then go back to his.

'Bill never liked Continental food. He liked his steak and chips, and this used to create a bit of a laugh sometimes when he couldn't make the foreign waiters understand what he wanted. I used to try to get him to eat frogs' legs and snails, but he wouldn't have any! He didn't drink when we first knew him, but we soon cured him of that habit!'

'We had some great times together. We were down in the South of France on holiday once, and on this particular occasion it was about 3 o'clock in the morning. There was nothing much to do so I went off to bed, but Billy said, "I'm going to stick around and find a bird." He couldn't believe his luck when he spotted this rather gorgeous blonde lady making eyes at him. She looked really nice, so he went over and started chatting her up. But somehow he didn't fancy her once he started talking to her . . . there was something very strange about her, but he wasn't quite sure what it was. Suddenly Bill realised – he'd been chatting up a bloke in drag! They do it very well down there, and old Billy had really been taken in for the first few minutes.'

Mike also said that he and Bill were really close friends and that they didn't fall out very often. However, on the few occasions they did row (which was usually over girls), Bill would never be the one to make it up. He would always wait for Mike to come round and see him. Mrs Ivy told Bill that he had too much pride. 'It's not that,' he told her, 'but if I go and see Mike and apologise, he'll probably think that I only want to know him because of his status and his money, like a lot of the others. He'll probably think that I'm not genuine – so I'll wait until he comes round.'

One of the lesser-known riders, Tony Blain, remembers an incident concerning Bill's attitude which occurred when he returned from the Continent after his first outings on the work Yamahas.

'When Bill first started getting his works-supported rides he seemed to be almost apologetic about it. We hadn't seen him for a while as he'd been away racing the Yamahas, and this was his first meeting back in England at Brands Hatch. We were all sitting on the lawn in front of the bar, all the old crowd, clowning around, laughing and telling jokes – our usual sort of carry-on. Then Bill came up, and we were all a little bit wary of him because he'd moved out of our class, and out of our circle as it were. None of us were quite sure how he would react to us. We weren't really sure how he would take it if we included him in the usual leg-pulling, and this seemed to hurt him – it was quite noticeable – because he then began to go out of his way to try to convince us that he was still the same old Bill.

'He was sitting just on the fringe of the circle, and when he joined-in and told a few jokes, we all laughed politely, but it didn't really work somehow. I remember him doing cartwheels and hand-stands, like he used to, in a desperate attempt to convince us that he hadn't changed. Really, it was all the rest of us who created this atmosphere, because we weren't sure whether he would still accept us. It was quite sad in a way, but it did show that Bill really did care about his old mates. After that it was just like old times again.'

Contrary to what some people thought, Bill did not have an inferiority complex about his size. When he was young he did have

G

a slight complex about being small when he first started going out with girls – he used to moan at them if they wore high-heeled shoes. But he overcame this problem by making a joke of his size. If he was at a dance or a party, he would ask the tallest girl there to dance with him. 'Hang on,' he would say, 'and I'll just go and get my stilts!' Later in life he claimed that being small was an advantage because he could fool people into thinking he was much younger, especially when he grew his hair long.

Possibly it was because of his size that he was so determined. Few people as small as Ivy have been any good at motorcycle racing, and certainly none have ever done as well. The odds were stacked against him, and he knew it, but he wouldn't admit it or accept it. Quite the opposite, he set out to show everyone that a little guy could do just as well as anyone else, better in fact. One person said of Bill, 'You never noticed him by his size, or by his mouth, but by what he did. Through his achievements he was a giant in everyone's eyes.'

As a youngster Bill didn't have the ability to converse with a crowd of people, and he wouldn't say a word to strangers. If there were several people in the house he would either go up to his room or go out. He hadn't the confidence to mix and talk with others, but as he grew up the problem disappeared.

Then, when he first started being successful he felt slightly inadequate. Socially, he felt out of place and a little inferior among the more educated people he came into contact with, but in time, he overcame this and could hold his own in any company. He would converse with anyone, but he was always fully aware of his lack of further education; he considered that he didn't have the brains to be really well educated, and he regretted it.

Through attending social functions as a guest of honour Bill was often asked to make a speech, and at first he hated it, but he persevered and developed into a reasonably good public speaker, though he never grew to enjoy it.

They thought the world of Ivy at Brands Hatch. From the management to the catering staff, little Bill was their favourite and Brands became his second home; even when he wasn't riding there he popped in quite often just to see everyone. He would amble into the various offices for a chat with the secretaries, or go into the kitchen for a natter with the ladies who worked in the café. He even took the barmaids out on a shopping spree once. Rosie, wife of George Officer, the track manager, remembers this incident clearly:

'One day, Bill gave Angie, one of the barmaids, and I a lift into town. We wanted to go shopping to buy some new gear, but he wasn't content just to drop us off and pick us up – Bill wanted to go shopping with us to see what we were going to buy! He really wanted to see what the dresses looked like, and he was a great one for knowing fashion. He'd pull a face if we walked out of the cubicle with something that didn't suit us. Even if it was fashionable if it wasn't quite 'us' he would say so. But he wouldn't be silly or laugh about it; he would give his candid opinion. In fact he was very helpful – he was very serious in the little things that most men don't understand. If some of the chaps in the bar had known that Bill had taken us out to buy a dress, they would probably have laughed their heads off, but it didn't worry him. If he could spare the time to help someone, he would.

'He used to be good fun in the bar, and when the clubhouse wasn't too busy the boys sometimes indulged in bets on press-ups and things like that, and up against all the big and manly-looking fellas Bill usually won. He was a great believer in what he did, and he was very sincere – it didn't matter what it was. He always spoke, even if he was surrounded by a crowd of birds, and if you were sitting alone in the corner he would involve you in the conversation. Bill enjoyed a good laugh if everybody was happy about it, but he would never see one person standing alone and being made the laughing stock. He had a terrific personality for one so small.'

Some people enjoy laughing and joking when they're making fun of somebody else, but they can't stand having their own leg pulled. Ivy was never like this, and he could laugh just as heartily if the joke was on him as if it was on someone else. There was a meeting at Brands Hatch one day, and people were given the opportunity of asking questions. Anthony Marsh, MCD's services manager, was present, and he explains what happened:

'Bill asked a question. The lighting wasn't very good, and the chap who was answering couldn't see where the voice was coming from, so he said, "Would you stand up, please." And without stopping to think I made a very silly old music hall joke. I said, "He's *already* standing up!" This went down very well with the audience, but tremendously well with Bill – he took it very well indeed. He was never self-conscious or offended if anyone pulled his leg about being small.'

Sometimes Bill would invite the Brands Hatch secretaries out for a drink at lunchtime, and one day, after a few of them had been drinking at a near-by pub, Bill challenged Tricia Wilcocksan, the general manager's secretary, to a race back to the circuit. He had the Stingray then, and when Bill got out into the car park he found he'd been blocked in. As he shunted to and fro in an effort to get out, all the girls piled into Tricia's Triumph Herald and roared off – and won. Bill had his leg pulled about that for a long time afterwards.

When he grew his hair long, the girls threatened to cut it, and one of them chased him round the office with a pair of scissors. 'You've got more hair than I have,' she said. 'Get orf woman,' shouted Bill in horror, 'you're not cutting my hair!' He really thought they meant it.

'He wasn't like a competitor,' said Tricia, 'he was more like a friend of everyone who worked at the circuit. He would walk into any office, and seemed to make a point of getting to know everyone. Mind you, he used to get a bit grumpy if we phoned him up early in the morning to discuss business. He had a standing order that if we wanted to phone him it had to be after 11 a.m. – or else!

Chris Lowe, MCD's general manager, said that Ivy was always very easy to negotiate with on a business level. 'He was always very fair. If we did a deal and he promised to turn up with two bikes, he would turn up with two bikes. He didn't go in for excuses; only in 1968, when he became incredibly mixed-up over all the Yamaha controversy, did he become a little difficult. His main crime on race day was parking his bloody great car in the road with the tape recorder running at full blast. He would be as pleasant as anybody in the morning, but by the afternoon, when the racing started, he would swear at me, or the officials, or anyone else. I think this was a sign of nerves.'

The disarming smile, the jovial manner, and the mischievous little laugh were the usual Billy, but like everyone else he had his faults. At times he could be obstinate, impulsive, eccentric and temperamental. There were some things that he didn't give a damn for, and he would defy officialdom rebelliously if he considered it unnecessary, or if it stood in his way. For example, he would tear along in his car, completely ignoring the restricted speed limits; he would park wherever he wanted to; and when he became famous he refused to carry a competitor's pass at race meetings. Consequently, many of the scrapes that he got into were of his own making.

At the 1966 Belgian Grand Prix, two policemen were on the gate and they were extremely officious. Despite being in his riding gear, and obviously a competitor, the coppers would not allow Bill into the pits because he wasn't carrying a pass. After trying to argue his way through, Bill tried to push his way in, only to be roughly manhandled and kicked by the policemen. That was too much and when Ivy lost his temper the Belgians got the shock of their lives as the 'midget' sailed into them with his fists flying like a miniature tornado. It was all the burly coppers could do to get Ivy into a near-by police van, in which, presumably, they intended to whisk him off to jail. Fortunately, one of the other riders saw what was going on, the organisers were fetched and the incident was smoothed over, but Bill had nobody to blame but himself. If he had carried a pass like everyone else, nothing would have happened. He always said, 'If they don't know who I am without having a blasted label stuck on me then they bloody well ought to!' Even after this incident he still refused to carry a pass, and continued to treat the little labels with the contempt he thought they deserved. At many foreign meetings the organisation borders on the realms of the ridiculous through people being over-officious, and it was inevitable that Ivy should be involved in other clashes, several of which ended in a punch-up.

Although Bill did things that he shouldn't have done, which obviously got him into trouble at times, he never *intended* to lose his temper – it just happened. One person said, 'It was best to be somewhere else if he lost his temper. He would go *absolutely berserk* for about two minutes, but he would cool off again just as quickly, and afterwards, he would apologise and be genuinely sorry. Then he would carry on as if nothing had happened, and even if he had been in the right he never bore a grudge.'

Ivy's indiscretions were never premeditated, they were committed in the heat of the moment, on impulse, and his unpredictable behaviour at race meetings can almost certainly be attributed to nervous tension, which rested like an indelicate finger on the hair-trigger of his temper. It was the little things which tended to upset him; things over which most people would not bat an eyelid could send Bill right off the deep end.

When Mrs Ivy was at Brands Hatch one day she overheard a spectator's remarks in the grandstand. Bill was on the Yamaha, and it wasn't running properly so he toured in to retire. The spectator, not realising that he was sitting virtually next to Bill's mother, said, 'Look at Ivy. Now he's a works rider he doesn't bother about putting on a good show at the smaller meetings.' Mrs Ivy was angry and upset, but she bit her tongue and said nothing. It would have been a waste of time trying to argue with someone obviously so ignorant, and she never mentioned it to Bill because she knew that it would have hurt him and made him very angry.

Because he was sensitive and emotional, Ivy was also vulnerable. He was very easily rattled, and it was as easy to hurt him with words as it was with actions. Sometimes, something which sparked off his temper on one occasion, could cast him into despondency on another. One could never be sure how he would react, and it was this ingredient in his character which made him unpredictable when things weren't running smoothly.

'Yes,' Mrs Ivy admitted, 'he could be very quick-tempered at times, and he was prone to get down-hearted quickly if things went wrong, but he could pull himself out of it just as quickly. He was never moody or sulky, but he was fairly highly-strung – a bit like Mike. Mind you, racers do live on their nerves.

'Another fault was that he strived too hard. He tried to do too much at times. He planned to write his own book, eventually, and it had to be his own – he didn't want anybody to ghost it. He was going to buy his own aeroplane, which he was going to fly himself – he didn't want anyone else to fly him. Whatever he did, he wanted to do it himself. He was too independent.'

Hand-in-glove with Bill's determination was his vitality; his 'boundless energy' Mrs Ivy called it. Although this was undoubtedly an asset, it was rather trying for the people around him, for most of them found that they couldn't move at the same pace as Bill. 'It was one of his biggest faults,' said Mrs Ivy, 'because he quickly lost patience with people who didn't work as he did. He didn't realise that others couldn't work at his tempo, and consequently he would become impatient. For instance, I might have suddenly remembered something that needed doing and remarked, "I really ought to do so and so." And he would say, "Well, do it now, Ethel." If he had anything to do he always did it there and then, even if it could have been left until another time, and he always expected everyone else to do the same. "Do it *now*," he always used to say. So I got wise to this, and if I planned to do anything I never told him, otherwise he would insist that it was done at the first available opportunity.

'He would be saucy at home sometimes, and his father would moan, but I used to say, "Never mind, I'd rather him be saucy at home and know how to behave himself in other people's houses, than him be an angel here and have other people say, "We don't want him in our house!"

'My relationship with Bill was much closer than a usual mother-and-son relationship, and he would discuss things with me that most sons wouldn't with their mothers. I didn't approve of some of the things that he did, but I didn't condemn him, as his father did; that's why Bill never told Ringo anything, because he knew he would moan. But I was always in his confidence, and I always listened to him – his father didn't know half the things he got up to! I'm glad that he enjoyed his life to the full, the way things turned out.'

Mrs Ivy had sometimes wished that her son had led a quieter life when he wasn't racing, but Bill's outlook on life was that he would enjoy the pleasant things while he could. 'I might never live to be old, so I might just as well enjoy myself,' he told her. Bill had never been able to picture himself getting old, and his mother had never known him to discuss what he would do when he reached middle-age, although he did once say that if he lived that long, then would be the time to think about it.

Contrary to the common belief held by a fair proportion of the older generation, young men with long hair are not dirty, scruffy individuals who don't see a bar of soap from one week to the next; the majority are probably far cleaner as well as much more appearance-conscious than their elders. Bill would get his sister to wash and blow-wave his hair, and he was forever taking baths. Ringo used to say, 'Good Lord – you're not having *another* bath? You had one this morning!' Bill would reply, 'I know, but I'm going out to dinner this evening.' Mr Ivy would shake his head, 'You're as bad as Ethel, she has a bath every day. It's bad for you, you shouldn't bath too often, it takes all the natural oils out of the skin!' But Bill didn't take a scrap of notice of this advice. 'Load of old rubbish,' he'd say with a laugh.

Although his mode of dress wasn't conventional, Bill would take a great pride in his clothes, and he never bought trash or junk. Every so often he would take a huge bundle of shirts and things down to his sister to be washed. 'My line used to look like a rainbow,' said Sue. 'He was very fussy about how I washed some of his shirts, too. He used to say, "Now, this one and this one must be washed by hand – if you put them through the machine you'll ruin 'em." I would put the whole lot through the washing machine, and when he collected them he would ask me if I'd washed the special ones by hand. I used to tell him that I had and he would be quite happy. It never made any difference how they were washed, but I never let on.'

Ask anyone who knew Ivy well what impressed them most of all about him, and most likely they would say, 'the way he looked after his parents'. People notice things like that, and to Bill, his home and family always came first. He enjoyed spending money on the things that he liked, but he also enjoyed spending out on some of the things that he knew his parents would like, yet never asked for. He helped his mum and dad buy a beautiful new detached bungalow, and that gave him more satisfaction than anything he ever bought himself. He always wanted to do as much as he could for Ethel and Ringo, and when his father developed heart trouble Bill told him, 'Don't worry about having to pack up work and wasting your time, I'll see that you never want for anything.'

Bill met Penny Allen, an attractive young model, through Mike Hailwood, and he started dating her regularly. 'When I first met him he was quite naïve in a refreshing sort of way,' Penny explained. 'I had been in London for some time, and I'd always led a certain kind of life among a certain kind of people, and Billy was so different. It was so nice to be with someone who could be impressed, because people today are so blasé. If we went to a new restaurant or something he would get so excited about things, whereas the people I had been used to, wouldn't. He wasn't a bit blasé which was lovely.

'Even in the short time I was with him, I noticed the difference in the way he could talk to people. When I first started going with him he felt terribly inadequate. When he first met my parents he was very lost for words, and he was frightened that what he was going to say wasn't going to be the right thing. Billy in the life that he had led had always said what he wanted to say, when he wanted to say it, and had been quite sure of himself, but when he started to travel and was living in London, he felt a little bit insecure and unsure of himself. You can't just barge in on people and be cocky, you've got to have a bit of reserve.

'He always used to say about himself, "I'm all mouth and trousers", and he was! If you met him you'd think he was so cocky, but I can remember being with him, and sitting with him, and he would talk about things and tears would come to his eyes. He was so emotional and so sensitive, and for a boy who appeared so cocky and self-sufficient he was terribly vulnerable. I think, for me, this was the nicest part about him; he was very lovable and very warm.

'I'd always been used to people who didn't tell you their true feelings, and they didn't lay their cards on the table, but Billy was so open. He used to say to me, "Well, this is what I feel, and I'm not going to pretend, even though you might think I'm silly for saying it", he was always so honest. After we'd been together literally a matter of weeks he said, "I've made up my mind . . .", whereas any other man . . . until the girl makes her feelings known he wouldn't dream of doing so.

'I'm very much a closed book, and I will never lay my cards on the table until somebody else has. But that was the marvellous thing about Billy, he was terribly sincere. He said, "Oh, you and your pride. You must always do the right thing," . . . "I'm not a bit like that, and I'm going to tell you what I think," which was so nice.

'At first, I must admit that he did embarrass me a little. Basically, I'm not shy, but reserved, and I like to do the right thing at the right time. We would be in a restaurant and Billy would say, "What's this, then?", very loud in front of the waiters and things like that, and it did embarrass me. Not that I cared, but I get embarrassed very easily, and I used to cringe under the table. But once I knew him it didn't make any difference at all.

'If we had a row he would get terribly depressed. He was like a little boy. I mean, he would really go to pieces and get very upset, and if it was my fault he would phone up and say he was sorry! He was so sweet. He sent me two dozen red roses once, saying that he was sorry, and the row was my fault. I felt so dreadful!

'Through living out in the country I think he led a very different sort of life. Not limited, but rather sheltered. Then, when he became successful and moved to London in the middle of it all he began to change. He learned a different way of life, and as he mixed with different people, so he became more worldly, but he was never blasé with it, and he still retained his modesty. He was getting himself an education all the time as far as everyday living was concerned.'

Unlike some competitors Bill was not superstitious. He didn't believe in good luck charms or black cats, he only believed in fate. He often said, 'When your number comes up – that's it', and he never believed in life after death. 'When you're gone, you're gone,' he would say. 'You just snuff it – and that's your lot.'

One day he was busy preparing a meal in his flat when there was a knock at the door. It was a woman with a pile of books and leaflets, who explained that she represented a certain religious cult. Bill said that he wasn't interested as he didn't believe in anything like that, but the woman was very persistent and started talking enthusiastically about her cause. Bill just stood there as she rambled on, but although he wanted to get rid of her he didn't like to be rude. Suddenly, there was a smell of burning coming from the kitchen, and Bill dashed off to find his dinner ruined. He returned to the woman at the door, and said, 'You really believe there's somebody up there?' The woman replied that she knew there was. 'Well, you've just convinced me that there isn't,' said Bill, 'because if there was he would have turned the stove off while I was standing here chatting to you, and my chips wouldn't have been burnt!'

8

The needle

UNDERSTANDABLY BILL was delighted about winning the world championship in 1967.

'I'm the happiest man in the world, everything has turned out so well for me. I've got the best car I could wish for, a nice flat, and there's enough money in the bank for me to go out to enjoy myself whenever I like.' Bill was talking to Mick Woollett of *Motor Cycle*, as he lounged in the comfort of a black-hide swivel chair – part of the furnishings of the luxury flat that he had bought from Mike Hailwood.

In his article, Woollett hinted that Ivy was the possible number-one choice for the 1968 season. Under the headlines 'BILL IVY NEW FIRST STRING FOR YAMAHA?', the article continued: 'Sporting a brand-new mod hairstyle, Bill eased his tiny yet stocky 5 ft 3 in frame in the chair when I suggested that part of his contentment with life was, if rumour is to be believed, that he and not Phil Read is to be the Yamaha first string in 1968.

'Obviously the new 125cc world champion would have preferred to dodge that question! But after giving it a good deal of serious thought he evasively replied, "Well, you can certainly say that my ambition is to score a double by winning both the 125 and the 250cc titles. I'll be trying very hard in both classes and the factory won't mind which rider wins so long as he's on a Yamaha."

'Not a direct answer, but one which indicates that Bill won't be shutting it off to let Phil Read win 250cc races as he did this year – notably at the Czech GP and at the Italian GP.'

Mick Woollett, a very shrewd journalist, certainly wasn't far off the mark, but Ivy didn't tell the whole tale – he was much too diplomatic for that. Very few people knew, but Yamaha's original team orders were that Ivy should lead the team, and that Yamaha wanted him to win both titles – *with Phil Read backing him up!*

One can imagine Read's reaction, for he had been in the team since 1963. He had been the captain, and always the undisputed number-one rider, during which time he had ridden many fine races for the Japanese concern, including winning the 250cc world titles in 1964 and 1965. Then, when Mike Hailwood (who had been riding in the bigger classes when he rode for MV Agusta) swopped camps and signed for Honda, Read lost his crown to the maestro in 1966 and 1967. Now he was extremely anxious to win it back, so it was understandable that he was bitterly disappointed when he discovered that he would not be allowed the opportunity of doing so.

Honda and Suzuki had already announced their intentions of withdrawing from the grand prix scene, and although Hailwood continued to ride Hondas in non-classic events, he had signed an agreement *not* to contest the world championships. So, with their main rivals out of the way, it was obvious that Yamaha, the last remaining Japanese works team, were a certainty for both 125 and 250cc championships; there were no other racing machines in the world capable of giving them a run for their money. There were only two horses in the race, Ivy and Read; the rest were also-rans. The only public interest which surrounded these classes at the beginning of the season was the mild speculation as to which rider was to win what. On paper the scene looked very dull, but as the season progressed a rift developed between the two riders, the team orders went out of the window, and a bitter feud between the pair set the races alight. The controversy stirred up more interest and received more publicity than the sport has ever known. Race fans flocked to the circuits in their thousands to witness the awe-inspiring spectacles of the Yamaha men striving desperately for victory. The Press dubbed the battles as 'grudge races', and the public cheered or booed, according to who they wanted to win. The FIM, who control the sport internationally, ordered an inquiry into people riding to orders, race organisers complicated the issue, and the Japanese shrunk away from the situation in sheer embarrassment.

How did it happen? Whose fault was it? Who was right and who was wrong? The public never knew the whole story, but here we shall endeavour to throw a little more light on what happened behind the scenes.

To a certain extent one can sympathise with Phil Read. He hadn't won a championship for two years, although he only failed by the narrowest of margins to wrest the 250 crown back from

Hailwood in 1967. Ivy had reaped the glory that year by winning the 125 title, and presumably this influenced the Japanese into wanting him to go for the double in 1968. When the two riders were informed of Yamaha's orders Ivy was delighted, but Read quite naturally was very upset. He protested and disputed them, so much so that Bill contacted Yamaha and suggested that the original orders be changed in favour of Phil winning the 125 events. The Japanese were reluctant to do so, for they really wanted Ivy to win both if he could, but they respected his sportsmanship and agreed.

Here it must be stated emphatically that Read had Ivy to thank for getting the team orders changed in his favour, and that he agreed to the plan. Ivy had told Yamaha, 'Let Phil Read win the 125 – I'll be happy with just the 250', and both riders signed their contracts on the understanding that each, where possible, was to let the other win his respective class. Read was to be number-one in the 125 class, and Ivy in the 250. These orders were never actually written into the contracts, for they would have contravened the FIM rules, but they were assurances given to their employers under a gentleman's agreement. Now, *if Phil Read had no intention of sticking to his part of the bargain, why did he agree to the orders and sign the contract, thereby inferring that he would stand by them?* Possibly because if he had further disputed Yamaha's plans there would have been a very good chance of him losing his place in the team altogether, and that would have entailed losing a great deal of money. Furthermore, there were no other works machines available which were capable of winning a world championship. An indication of who the Japanese favoured was the fact that Ivy alone was summoned to Japan to test the new 1968 machines in March.

Bill exploded into action in the first grand prix at Nurburgring in West Germany, not only on the bikes but also in another of his brushes with officialdom. As the long-haired little figure strutted out to the pit area a burly official stopped him and demanded to see his pass. Needless to say, Bill wasn't carrying one, but he argued his way through and then went to the race office to ask the organisers to tell the chap on the gate to stop hindering him. This was done, but later, when he tried to get out on to the circuit for the final practice session, despite being in riding gear this time and walking behind his machine which was being wheeled out by a mechanic, the official again refused to let Bill through. He blocked the entrance and was most obstinate – no pass, no admittance. Ivy, his temper rising, warned the fellow that if he didn't get out of his way he would 'thump him'.

The official stood his ground, defiantly . . . then collapsed like a sack of potatoes as Ivy floored him with a right hook! People who saw the incident say that it was like something out of 'The Keystone Cops'. As the big German sprawled on the ground, little Bill sprinted down to the pit area, pursued by a whole army of policemen and officials. They captured him and marched him in front of the race organisers, who said, 'Herr Villiam Ivy, you must not do this – it is not how a gentleman should behave.' To which Bill replied that he wasn't 'a —— gentleman, anyway', and claimed that he was being victimised because of his long hair, which apparently didn't go down at all well with the Germans.

The team orders were carried out satisfactorily when Phil won the 125cc race – Bill stopped with a broken crankshaft – and in the 250 event the former pulled out with an over-heated engine, leaving Bill to win at record speed.

At the Spanish round, fate stepped in and took a hand in the situation. Both riders retired in the smaller class with broken crankshafts, and Phil won the 250 after Bill had stopped with ignition trouble.

It was in the Isle of Man when the needle first began to creep in. Phil told Bill that he 'wasn't going to hang around and wait in the 250 race'. Bill just shrugged his shoulders and didn't say a lot about it. He was upset, but he didn't want any trouble in the Yamaha camp. His main concern was that if any problems arose, Nieto, the likeable little Japanese who was in charge of team organisation might get into trouble with the factory chiefs in Japan.

Before the race the atmosphere in the team began to change, and Read first tried psychological warfare on his rival. He had tried Dunlop's new wide-section tyre during the final stages of practice, and Bill had asked him what it was like because when he tried the tyre it had been wet, and he hadn't been able to draw a satisfactory comparison. Phil said that the tyre was no good and that the standard one was much better, so the smaller tyres were fitted to both machines for the race.

When race day came and all the riders and machines were in the warming-up area, Phil suddenly said, 'Nieto – I want the big tyre put on!' Poor Nieto. It was almost unheard of for him to lose his temper, but he flew into a terrific tantrum and shouted and raged at Phil. There was a big row about it and a big panic session trying to change the wheel in time.

In all probability the tyre was no better, and it appeared that Read was trying to make a big scene in order to put Ivy off, by making him think that the big tyre was better and that he was at a disadvantage. 'Gamesmanship' is the term which is used to describe these 'off-putting' tactics which, unfortunately, seem to be the order rather than the exception in so many professional sports these days.

However, it backfired on this occasion for it stung Ivy into riding as hard as he could, and he was in stupendous form. He shattered Mike Hailwood's lap record from a standing start to notch a fantastic 105·51 mph, which was even more outstanding when it was discovered that his machine was a full 7 mph slower than the previous year – he only recorded 144 mph through the speed trap!

At the end of the first lap he led his 'team-mate' by 14 seconds, but on the second lap the exhaust system began to disintegrate, his Yamaha slowed, and at the end of the third lap Read led by 14 seconds. There were more problems ahead for Bill, and while hurtling through the flat-out curves at Milntown he caught his right foot underneath the footrest, wrenched his ankle and tore a gaping hole in his boot. Read was in trouble, too, and he retired on the following lap with a puncture. It would have been poetic justice if it had been the front tyre, which had been changed, but in fact, it was the back one.

Although in considerable pain, Ivy nursed himself and his ailing machine home to victory. He could hardly walk, so he was carried barefoot to the winners' rostrum, the discarded remains of his right boot bearing testimony to the effort he had made on his winning ride. That evening, when the jubilant victor was out on the customary celebration spree, dancing with all the dollies, one of the boys said, 'I see your foot's all right now, Bill!' With his impish grin, Bill gave the girl he was dancing with a little cuddle. 'Ah yes,' he said, 'pussy cures everything!'

Annoyed over Phil's threats to flout team orders, Bill decided to give his 'team-mate' a scare in the 125cc event. He didn't tell anyone, but he hadn't the slightest intention of disobeying team orders. His plan was to go flat-out to gain the lead and fox Phil into believing that he intended to win, then ease up during the last few miles of the race.

From the drop of the flag both men screamed their tiny machines round the circuit at a searing pace. Read rode desperately in an effort to gain the lead, but at the end of the first lap he trailed Ivy by four seconds. Then Ivy really opened the taps and hurtled round at an incredible speed for a 125, intent on breaking the magic 100 mph barrier. Reports came in from around the course that he was flying, and one spectator who was standing at the bottom of Barregarrow said that Ivy streaked down the hill standing on the footrests, wrestling with the bike in an effort to control a terrifying 'tank slapper'. Apparently the front wheel was flapping about all over the place, and the bike was doing its best to tie itself in a knot, but Ivy didn't shut down a scrap – he just stood up and fought it with the throttle wide open at around 130 mph!

Read was doing his best to top the 'ton' as well, but the mechanics had purposely set up his machine for reliability, which had taken the fine edge off the performance. Realising this, he gave the mechanics an angry sign as he flashed past the pits to begin his final lap. Despite this, he recorded a lap at 99·76 mph.

It was left to Ivy to break that seemingly impossible barrier, and break it he did. He reeled off his second lap at 100·32 mph, a truly fantastic performance, and he led the race by over 11 seconds. At this point in the race the Yamaha mechanics became very worried; was Bill going to slow up to let Phil win or wasn't he? One of the mechanics was sent up to Governor's Bridge, about 500 yards from the finish, with a pit board and stopwatches, and orders to stop Ivy if he was still leading on corrected time, and make him wait long enough to ensure that Read could win.

There was no need for concern, though, for as much as Bill *wanted* to win, he had no intention of going against Yamaha's wishes. He slowed-up in the closing miles of the race, and to the astonishment of spectators at Creg-ny-Baa, the cheeky imp cut his engine and stopped to ask who was winning! This action left no doubt in anyone's mind that the Yamaha men *were* riding to orders, even though it could never be factory policy publicly to announce this. So Bill toured in to finish almost a minute behind Phil, and nearly nine minutes ahead of third finisher Kel Carruthers on a Honda production racer.

The same question was on everybody's lips, especially the gentlemen from the Press – did Bill Ivy swing the race or not? Of course, Bill denied that he had and claimed that his engine had gone off-song on the last lap, this statement being accompanied by the familiar Ivy grin, so that even an imbecile would have doubted its truth. Everyone 'knew' that he had eased-up to let Read win.

Whether Bill's actions pricked Phil's conscience or not it's difficult to say, but there is no doubt that he let Ivy win the 250cc race in Holland. There was only one-tenth of a second between them at the finish, and their high-speed exhibition had the crowd on its toes. In the 125 event Bill only completed two laps before retiring. He'd injured his other foot – another rider had ridden over it at the start – so whilst Read sped on to victory Ivy was taken to hospital for medical attention.

Again it was fate, that fickle master of so many situations, which decided the outcome of the Belgian GP, where there was no 125 round. Ivy shot into the lead in the 250 race as Read's bike refused to run properly on its four cylinders. The race seemed to be cut-and-dried, but poor Bill cursed his luck when his mount developed ignition trouble and he pulled in to retire. Stopping for a plug change had left Phil way down the field, but he rode magnificently to catch Rod Gould (Yamaha-Bultaco) and Heinz Rosner (MZ) on the last lap to win. But Bill had made the fastest lap at 125·35 mph.

The orders were adhered to at the East German round, when Bill faked the need for a plug change after the first lap of the 125 race, then tore round to beat everybody except Phil, and in doing so establish a new lap record. In the 250 Phil did the same; he stopped to top-up his radiator (which was already full), and then shot off in pursuit. He went so quickly that he caught Bill up again, and after two more laps of skirmishing followed the Maidstone lad over the line a mere tenth of a second behind.

To the uninitiated, team riding might appear to be cheating the public by not giving them a 'genuine' race, but this was never so in Read's and Ivy's case; they rode as hard as they could and played a high-speed game of cat-and-mouse. If they had wanted to they could have gone far slower and still trounced everyone else, but they were too professional for that. Records tumbled at nearly every circuit as the pair genuinely pitted their wits against each other. Usually, it was only during the last dash for the finishing line that one would ease up a fraction to ensure that the other took the chequered flag. It was done so cleverly that if there hadn't been a feud, which threw everything into the open, most people would never have guessed that the Yamaha men were not racing all the way for real. But the rivalry was beginning to warm up, and although the team orders were still being met, neither man was enjoying letting the other win.

As the season wore on it became more or less a certainty that Yamaha would pull out of racing at the end of the year. After the TT they had called all but two of their mechanics back to Japan, and after the Czechoslovakian GP they, too, were to return, leaving both riders to arrange their own personal mechanics in preparing

H

and maintaining the complicated, temperamental four-cylinder machines. Phil enlisted the help of Roy Robinson, and Bill had Ron Eldridge to help him, both the English mechanics having been working with the Japanese in readiness for the time when they would take over.

After the East German round Read was leading in the 125cc championship with four wins, and in the 250 class Ivy topped the table with four wins to Read's two wins and two seconds. Only four rounds remained in Czechoslovakia, Finland, Ireland and Italy. In the smaller class a rider's five best performances counted, so as Read already had four wins he needed only one more to clinch the championship. In the 250 class the six best results counted from a total of ten rounds, and Read knew that he could still take that title as well, *if he rode to win!*

By the time of the Czechoslovakian GP it was a foregone conclusion that Yamaha had no intention of running a works team the following season. Consequently, Read knew that he would be out of a job at the end of the year, anyway, so what had he to lose by disobeying Yamaha's orders and going all-out for both titles? He knew that it would not jeopardize his chances of being selected for the team again, because there would be no team, so he decided to go his own way in an effort to reap all the glory for himself.

When Bill first joined the team Mike Duff had warned him not to let Phil Read dominate him. Speaking of Phil, Mike said: 'I liked him as a person and as a rider, but he had some funny ideas, and a funny sense of humour. His humour in most cases was greatly misunderstood, but his riding talents were far from misunderstood, he was an extremely aggressive rider on almost every circuit.

'Read and I never really hit it off too well, and I found the pressure of riding as second-string to him very trying. Read was out for Read and nobody else, and he always said, "I can cry on the way to the bank!"

'His favourite trick was his insistence in entering us both for non-classic events as 'Yamaha Racing Team', for which he would do all the financial arrangements. He would ask how much I would like to compete at Brands, for example, and I might say that I'd accept £120 for one start; he'd then organise £300 to £350 for the team, give me what I asked for and keep the rest. I agreed that he was worth more than me, but I felt very secondhand doing business in this manner. This is basically what I warned Bill against.

'Bill was easily led and during his first season as a full team member he obviously relied a great deal on Phil Read's experience. I believe this to be where the trouble started. As Bill learned he was able to see where he was being taken for a ride, and the end result was the bitter controversy in 1968.'

As people, Read and Ivy were totally different, and their characters were opposite to the extreme. Their only similarity was their riding skill, but even their individual determination to succeed could be put into entirely different categories. For example, as much as Bill *wanted* to beat Phil in the 125 events, because he had given his word to let Phil win he stuck by it, whereas Phil's solitary aim seemingly was to be successful, and sentiment wasn't allowed to stand in his way. The fact that Yamaha, who paid him, and were relying upon him under a gentleman's agreement to comply with their wishes, and Ivy, the very person who had handed him the 125 title on a plate, were the ones who stood between him and the 250 title didn't make a scrap of difference – success was all that mattered. Read, a hard and shrewd businessman, a clever and intelligent operator, was out for 'number one', and he was intent on clinching the double, whether they liked it or not.

However, Phil did not inform Ivy of his intentions until *after* he had won the 125 race and secured the championship in Czechoslovakia. If Bill had known *before* the race he would almost certainly have ridden to win, and there was an outside chance that he could have stopped Phil taking the title. As it happened, Bill crashed heavily on the wet Brno circuit and was carted off to the first-aid centre while Read sped on to win his first ultra-lightweight world championship.

Apart from hurting his leg and receiving a few bumps and bruises, Bill was okay, and later in the afternoon, as he lined up for the 250 race, Phil told him that he would be racing to win. All along Bill had suspected that Read was up to something, and somehow he guessed how it was going to be. Read really meant business, too, that day and although Ivy strived to catch him he was hampered by a faulty front brake and finished several seconds behind.

After the race Ivy stormed angrily into the Yamaha pit and accused Read of not playing the game. A bitter argument followed, and Read said that he was 'fed up with slowing down to let Ivy win'. The bubble had burst, and the clash of personalities inevitably had come to a head. The controversial feud had begun, and the team-mates became heated rivals, almost enemies.

The situation received maximum publicity in the Press, and this created a tremendous amount of public interest. It became the main topic of conversation amongst the racing fraternity, and even people who normally didn't follow the sport were taking a keen interest in what was going on.

Yamaha threatened to take Read's bikes away from him, to which he replied, 'If I can't ride to win I'll quit.' The FIM ordered an inquiry into the fiasco and stated that if, at any time, it was proved that either rider slowed down purposely to let the other win action would be taken. The organisers of the Ulster GP required assurances from Yamaha that both Ivy and Read would be free to ride unrestricted races at their meeting, and the whole crazy situation became even more complex. Yamaha were ordering Read to let Ivy win, and the FIM warned him that if he did he would be in trouble!

One week after the flare-up, *Motor Cycle* published the following quote by Phil Read: 'Having stuck my neck out to help develop the Yamaha fours, I want an equal chance now that they're good. If Bill reckons he can beat me, let him prove it!'

Asked for his views, Ivy replied: 'I don't know what Phil's moaning about. I've let him win the 125 title; why shouldn't he let me win the 250 class? The only reason I fell off in Czecho' was because I slowed down to follow him. I only wish this business had happened earlier in the year, then we would have found out who was the better rider.'

Phil's actions had appalled Bill, and he became fanatically determined to prove that he could win the championship on his own merit. But the battle of wits, the psychological warfare, and the electrifying atmosphere had the effect of putting him constantly on edge. He was sensitive and Phil knew this and played on it.

Read was far better equipped for the situation than Ivy. He had the benefit of a better education, he was more intelligent, and he was a much more experienced tactician. On top of that, his whole psychological outlook enabled him to cope better than Bill. He was thicker-skinned, unaffected by other people's comments, and unlike his rival was comparatively cool, calculating, and virtually unflappable.

Consequently, once the feud had developed Ivy was at a distinct disadvantage. He strove too hard, he was too forceful, and consequently his riding became ragged. He had lost that vital rhythm, that finesse which enables a rider to race smoothly and predictably on the limit. The previous year, and up to the time of his discontentment in 1968, Bill had been riding fractionally better than Phil.

But now Read was on top of his form, was superbly confident, and with the 125 title already under his belt the sweet smell of success was urging him on.

So the battle moved to the next arena – Imatra, the picturesque, tree-lined home of the Finnish GP. Here Ron Eldridge recounts the story:

'Normally the bikes would do two or three grand prix races on one set of crankshafts, but as soon as the needle started Bill insisted on having a new crank fitted before every race. His idea was to rev the bike 1,000 rpm higher in the hope that a new crank would stand up to it and last the distance. We'd do the practice on the crankshafts that had been used for the previous race, then put a brand-new set in the night before the event. This meant going out for the race without trying the bike, so everything had to be spot-on; it was a big job and it involved a lot of hard work.

'Roy Robinson and myself had spent a whole fortnight in Hamburg, completely rebuilding the bikes in readiness for the Finnish GP, so when we arrived in Finland we set the garage up, put the numbers on the bikes, and were all organised for practice.

'Bill flew in from England with a large parcel and a bloody great box. He'd brought some new crankshafts with him, and a complete set of Norton forks to go on the 250. The forks had been converted to fit his private 250 to improve the handling, and he thought that if he took them off and fitted them on his GP bike it would give him an advantage over Phil.

'Well, before Bill arrived, Yamaha had sent us a telegram saying, "DO NOT USE CRANKSHAFTS SUPPLIED AT HAMBURG". Apparently they were faulty. I was certain that the crank I'd put in was from the original old stock, and was all right, but Bill wasn't! He wanted me to put *another* new set of crankshafts in, just for practice, and convert the bike to take the Norton forks. Well, I'd already done a lot of work in Hamburg, and what with the drive up to Finland the last thing I felt like doing was any more work. "No," I thought to myself, "I'm going to stick to my guns." So I said to Bill, "No – the bike's *right*, and it's ready for practice. *I'm* doing the bike and I say it's *right*!" Roy Robinson agreed with me that it wasn't necessary to change the crankshafts.

'To say the least Bill and I had a barney about it, in fact we had a blazing row. He got very angry. "If I want it done, *I bloody well want it done*!" he said, stamping his feet and jumping about. Roy was disgusted with him for making such a big scene about it, but it didn't seem to matter what we said, Bill had made up his mind. "Look," he said, "if you don't do it – and you're supposed to be the mechanic – *I'll do the bloody thing*!" So I said, "Okay then, off you go – let's see you."

'And he would have done – he really would have done it himself! As soon as he started to get ready to make an attempt at it, I thought, "Crikey, he means it, so *I'd* better do it."

'It meant working right through the night, and going straight up to practice the following morning. It was a hell of a lot of work. Changing the crank wasn't too bad as I'd done it lots of times before, but putting the forks on was a really fiddly job. We got the original ones off, put the Norton ones on, but they wouldn't fit properly. The frames were different on the GP bikes, and no matter what we did we just couldn't stop the forks fouling the frame when the steering was turned. We tried altering various pieces but it made no difference – it couldn't be done. So we had all that work for nothing and had to swop back to the original set-up.

'But the thing that impressed me about Bill was his attitude. If I had refused to do it he was prepared to have a go all by himself. Afterwards, when the bike was finished, we went and had a drink together. That's what I liked about him; we could have a flaming row one minute and be the best of friends again the next. He never bore a grudge and would forget all about it, carrying on as if nothing had happened, and despite our ups and downs he always appreciated what was done for him. You couldn't over-emphasize how much he thought of the Japanese mechanics, and they thought the world of him. Bill would always thank them, and take them out for a meal or show his appreciation in some way.'

Unfortunately, Bill's efforts in Finland were all in vain. While sitting on Phil's tail in the 125cc race, his front brake lost its adjustment and he was forced to make a 45-second pit stop to rectify the trouble. After that he had no hope of catching the leader, but he had the consolation of setting up a new lap record over 3 seconds faster than the old one held by Taveri.

The rain bucketed down for the 250 event, and for the first nine laps Read was content to sit on Ivy's tail, then he made his effort and nipped past. Bill was determined not to be shaken off, for he was in a fighting mood, but that was his downfall for he tried too hard and came off. While Phil cruised on to win, Bill was carried off on a stretcher with a suspected broken leg. At first it seemed as if the injury would put him out of the title chase, but an X-ray examination revealed only a splintered bone – not serious enough to keep the 'iron man' out of the saddle, but painful none the less. Ivy limped on to Ulster.

With his lack of experience of the 7·4-miles Dundrod circuit (he'd only raced there once), Bill was not very optimistic about his chances. However, in the 125 event he and Phil scorched round together until the latter shot up a slip road, leaving Bill to win by 2·6 seconds. Between them they smashed the lap record no fewer than nine times, and eventually it went to Read in his attempt to catch Bill again, at an incredible 102·44 mph.

Both riders had been worried about their machines' capabilities of completing the 250 race without taking on fuel. A pit stop was out of the question, but to risk using the standard Yamaha fuel tank only to run out of petrol during the closing stages of the race would have been sheer folly, so each rider, unbeknown to the other, had a special outsize fuel tank made, just for that one race. It must have been quite a surprise for each of them when they discovered that the other had had the same idea!

Shortly before the start of the 250 race, rain swept across the circuit, and things looked black for Ivy; he had fallen in the wet during the two previous GPs, and this naturally hadn't increased his confidence. Of the two, Read was the better rider in the wet, and this, coupled with his superior knowledge of the track, made him a firm favourite to clinch the race that would make him a double world champion for the first time.

The flag dropped and the field streaked off in a cloud of spray, with the Yamaha pair in their usual places at the front. Ivy, riding with all his old confidence and smooth style, followed in Read's wheel-tracks, and when the roads began to dry he forged ahead. As Read chased after the leader, a stone flung up from Ivy's rear wheel punctured his radiator, and after all the water had run out the engine eventually seized. As Phil cursed his luck William cruised jubilantly home to victory.

The pendulum seemed to be swinging in Ivy's favour now, for with five wins to Phil's four, the latter could not take the title with anything less than a win in the final round in Italy, and the super-fast Monza track suited Bill admirably. His light weight was a definite advantage where the Yamahas could be given their head on straights, and his machine usually would be noticeably quicker than Read's. On paper Ivy was the favourite, but in racing anything can happen, and as Monza drew near the interest and speculation grew. The feud had almost reached its climax, for the outcome of just one more race would decide who was to be the new 250cc champion of the world.

When the controversy first blew up, a lot of people thought it was a publicity stunt arranged by Ivy and Read to promote interest in their racing, but both riders denied this emphatically. 'I've got a grudge against Phil – there is no fix about it,' said Bill. 'He says he can beat me – let him prove it,' was Read's war cry. There was certainly nothing fixed about it. Each was convinced that he was the better man, and each was determined to prove it. It was a genuine war between them, and although it provided the public with a series of thrilling spectacles, there is no denying that it was an extremely dangerous situation.

Behind the scenes it was a weird set-up, more akin to fantasy than fact. Both machines would be prepared in the same garage, with Roy working on Phil's bikes on one side, and Ron fettling Bill's on the other, and both the riders would be there with them. Consequently, the rivals saw a lot of each other and it created a very strange atmosphere, one which Ron Eldridge could never really understand. Here is how he tried to explain it:

'They obviously saw a lot of each other, and surprisingly they got on quite well considering the circumstances. Phil is an easy bloke to get on with in some ways; he's well mannered and very polite. The funny thing was, they could go out and have a real needle with each other, come in and swear about each other (not *to* each other but *about* each other) after a race or practice, then during the evening they would be reasonably pleasant to one another. This was something I could never quite understand. Away from the tracks they tolerated each other – I'm sure they didn't like each other, but they put up with each other. The real battle of wits started at the circuits. But just before Monza the feud even began to creep into the preparation of the bikes as the vast stock of spares began to dwindle and there was only just enough of the vital parts to go round.

'Most of the time, the feud had Bill on edge and put him out of his stride. The bikes had to be set-up for each individual circuit, and if I did this according to Yamaha's chart (which was based on previous knowledge gained from racing on the same circuits), Bill frequently wanted to try different settings in an effort to find a better combination. At one meeting, after I'd prepared the 250 according to the chart, Bill suddenly decided that he wanted everything changed. There were so many combinations: Different fork yokes for altering the fork trail; different fork widths; spacers for adjusting the head angle; springs of varying poundage; and three different damper strengths – not including top dampers. Then there were the various grades of oil that could be used to give the forks a stiffer or softer action. So I changed everything according to Bill's instructions, but it wasn't right, and systematically we worked through practice altering everything again. He'd try the bike, come in and say it was too hard or too soft, then we'd change something and off he'd go again. Finally he was satisfied – but when I checked the settings to compare them with those on the chart they were exactly the same! So at least he must have known how to set up a bike! If there hadn't been a feud he would have had the bike prepared according to the chart and left it at that, but with all the controversy and with so much at stake, he was constantly looking for that fraction extra which might have given him some marginal improvement; really, he was looking for the impossible. The situation was playing on his nerves and he was thinking about it too much.'

And so to Monza, where the intense rivalry turned to bitter hatred, resentment and protests over petty trivialities. Before the race, Bill heard that if he won Phil planned to lodge an official protest. Phil obviously knew that Bill did not comply with the FIM minimum-weight ruling, and if he was beaten it was said that he planned to protest about this to try to get Bill disqualified. When Ivy got wind of this, he chased round and got some lead, weighed-up the correct amount, and strapped it to his machine to comply with the regulations. But the whole thing sickened him so much that he decided to find something to protest about if Read won. Whether it was Phil's intention to protest or whether it was merely an off-putting tactic in the psychological war it is difficult to determine, but it certainly had an effect on Bill. He flew into a rage and the angry, bitter remarks he made about his 'team-mate' were, to say the least, totally unprintable.

Battle commenced in the 125 event, and on a patchy track, half-dry from the overnight rain, Ivy and Read tore round as if they were glued together. This time it was Phil's turn to bite the dust. Following Bill round a corner on the penultimate lap, he overdid it and the little Yamaha skated from underneath him. Luckily he wasn't injured, and he was so far in front of the third man that he was able to kick his machine straight, remount and still finish second on two cylinders.

After the lunch break came the long-awaited needle match, the 250cc championship decider. From the start Read screamed his Yamaha into the lead, with Ivy in hot pursuit. For three laps they circulated together, then Ivy decided to blast by and he tried to overtake Read round the outside on the treacherous Curva Parabolica but again he was too determined. He lost control, shot on to the grass verge, the Yamaha bucking wildly, and only just managed to stay on board. By the time he'd sorted himself out Read was ten seconds to the good, and Bill's machine had oiled a plug, so it was only functioning on three cylinders. He lost ground steadily, and had a job to coax his machine home in second place, almost two minutes behind an overjoyed Read.

While the new world champion basked in the glory of his victory, a dejected Ivy walked over to the race office to lodge his protest. It was a feeble protest, made in confusion and resentment as an act of disgust. The only things he could think of regarding the legality of Read's machine were that the front number plate (which was identical to his own), did not comply with the regulations, and that the footrests were not completely ball-ended. He also claimed that Read had used a make of chain different from that which he had been under contract to use. It was obvious that such protests would not be upheld, and inevitably they were overruled by the clerk of the course after a short debate.

However, Ivy's actions stirred up a load of criticism in the Press, and some journalists made scathing remarks about his stupidity and bad sportsmanship. As a result, he lost a lot of sympathy from his fans over losing the title that rightfully should have been his. Letters were written to the Press, some defending Bill, others condemning his actions and running him down, and the conflict ended as it had begun, in a blaze of publicity.

With five wins and two second places apiece, the title had to be decided on time. Each rider's total race times were added up in the four races in which both had finished and Read's total of 3 hours 15 minutes 22·9 seconds, compared with Ivy's 3 hours 17 minutes 28·2 seconds to give him an advantage of 2 minutes 05·3 seconds with which to clinch the championship.

Apart from the publicity which the feud itself received, a lot of people were asking the question, 'Is team riding a good or bad thing for the sport?' In an article in *Motor Cycle* three of the world's most famous motorcyclists were asked for their opinions on the subject.

The great Stanley Woods said: 'The man who pays the piper

calls the tune. So manufacturers, who spend many thousands of pounds on racing, must be able to demand a certain amount of team discipline.' Although Stanley agreed that it was necessary, he personally did not approve of the practice.

Geoff Duke commented: 'From a manufacturer's point of view, riding to orders is a must. The only real point is how obvious you make it to the fans. The Moto-Guzzi men always rode as a team and they were past-masters of the art. They always made it look like a tremendous battle and everyone was happy. On the other hand I remember that when I was with the Norton team, one rider was told that because of the championship position he had to finish second. He went like a ding-bat until two laps from the end and then sat up and toured. He just had to make it obvious to the crowd what was happening. This sort of action makes a farce of the race and everyone knows what's going on.

'Personally, I don't like the idea of riding to orders unless it is essential. For example, it could be that a world championship is at stake. In the case of Yamaha, I think that Read and Ivy should have been given their heads. They are both experienced and it was obvious that barring some sort of disaster, Yamaha were a must to win both championships in the 125 and 250cc classes. So there was really no point in issuing orders. It would have been a different matter if they were facing a strong rival team. It's a bit ridiculous for the FIM to state that there shall be no riding to orders. This is a matter for the manufacturers concerned.'

Mike Hailwood had very strong views on the subject. He said, 'When you've got a team with two riders of similar ability, they must ride to orders – otherwise they would be falling off and blowing the bikes up in an effort to beat one another.'

In another article which appeared in *Motor Cycle News* later that year, Mike wrote: 'Poor old Bill always seems to get the hard end of the deal. He was quite entitled to be as upset as he was after the nasty trick that was played on him during all that upset with his so-called team-mate. I know I'd have felt just the same about it. Bill has been criticised for his protest about the size of Phil's number plate at the Italian Grand Prix. As far as Bill was concerned this was an act of final desperation. He had taken all he was prepared to and he was beginning to hit back. And in all the upset between the two Yamaha men, Bill was the one who didn't lose face with the Japanese.'

When interviewed, Mike elaborated on his views and said, 'Well, looking at it from a semi-outsider's point of view, I think that Phil

Read pulled a rotten trick. Bill had hung back to let him win 125cc races and Read went on to take the championship. Then Phil wouldn't let Bill win the 250 races and decided to try to win that title as well, which I thought was totally unfair. In my opinion Read was wrong – it's something I would never have done.

'The same type of situation existed in the Honda team with Jim Redman and I. I agreed to let Jim win the 500cc races and he agreed to let me win the 250 and 350cc events – and we stuck by it. I expect I could have beaten Jim in the 500, and he could probably have beaten me on occasions in the 250 and 350. But it was something that was mutually agreed between us, and that was it – we both stuck by it. And I think Phil should have stood by his agreement with Bill.'

But what of the other side of the coin? There are always two sides to every story, and it is only fair to record what Phil Read had to say on the matter in his book *Prince of Speed*, published in 1970 by Arthur Barker Ltd.

'Towards the end of 1968 I had good reason to believe that Yamaha would follow the other big Japanese factories by withdrawing from the grand prix scene. I had repeatedly raised this question with the factory chiefs in Japan, but had always received negative answers.

'I had started thinking a lot about my future – and the past. I was looking back on my first links with Yamaha, when their first grand prix offensive began. How I had helped nurse their early twin-cylinder machines into world-beaters, against far stronger opposition than existed towards the end of their world championship bid. The loss of the 250 crown was still foremost in my mind.

'I believed that Yamaha would withdraw from racing, and I desperately wanted this last chance of recapturing, if I could, the 250 world championship. Bill had a fair chance to beat me, having a few points in hand in the championship table. I obeyed Yamaha's wishes until we reached the Czechoslovakian Grand Prix – then I had to make up my mind about that 250 title.

'I knew it was now or never. I knew that I had found my old winning form again. Bill knew it, too, although he often joked about blowing me off at any time. I knew my contract, which I had with Yamaha, made no reference to agreeing to finish second to any rider. Of course, it dare not. If it had done it would have contravened the FIM code. I also knew that if I rebelled in Czecho', and won the 250, I would still leave Bill with a two point lead. Surely that was fair?

'After Czechoslovakia they called me "Read the Rebel". My decision not to slow up in the race and allow Bill to win caused one hell of a controversy. From Tokyo came angry warnings about my stubborn conduct, followed by threats to take my racing bikes away from me unless I agreed to ride to orders.

'I told Yamaha that I intended to ride to win in the remaining 250 world championship rounds – otherwise I would quit the team. I also made it quite clear to them that I was willing to climb down, if they assured me that I would be given the chance to win back the 250 title in 1969.

'They answered, saying, in effect, that if I did not do as I was told they would take the Yamaha works machines away from me. I replied repeating my demands, that I was not prepared to finish second and asking for confirmation from them that they would be competing in the next year's classics. I told them that if they wanted to take the bikes away from me they could do so any time they wished.

'There was no confirmation from them about their plans for the 1969 championships. But they did ask me to keep good relations with Bill. So, I reckoned it was certain that 1968 was to be the last for Yamaha.

'So I took the big plunge. I did what I thought was right. I have not changed my mind – I made Bill fully aware of my decision, and I left him with a fair chance of beating me in the remaining rounds of the championship.

'Yamaha had been spending immense sums of money on their racing. In return they wanted the maximum of success and publicity. I am sure, that in 1968, Bill and I gave them a finale that was brimful of both.'

What did the Japanese think about the outcome of the controversy? They were obviously embarrassed by it all, as Nieto, acting as spokesman for Yamaha, explained in his economical English with his quaint oriental accent:

'Bill's character was straight. He was a very good boy, nice guy – I like very much. In 1968, we decide team order is; 125 and 250 is Bill – Bill is fast. But Bill suggest give 125 to Phil. Then, at Czechoslovakian Grand Prix, Phil change this. He want team order cancelled. Then Bill try too hard – every time too hard. Everywhere he try too much to win, and Phil win both championships. Yamaha wish that Phil win only 125 and Bill 250, but Phil, he don't.'

Nieto went on to say that he really enjoyed working with Bill, especially when he took him out on the town, treated him to slap-up meals, and gave him a good time socially. He said that Bill made him laugh 'everytime', and that he was always amused when the little chap roared off the line with the front wheel of his Yamaha pawing the air. 'He try at race, always, to start upright,' said Nieto with a grin. 'Our 250 was very difficult handling, so he try every-thing – new ideas. So we must make his order, and I think by 1968 our racer is very good handling. I think he made it complete – he was very good suggest.'

According to Nieto, although Bill really enjoyed going to Japan, where he worked hard testing the bikes, he did not like the Japanese food – but he liked the girls! Also, by 1968 he had begun to pick up a little of the Japanese lingo.

It was in the Isle of Man, during TT week in 1970, when I inter-viewed Nieto. We sat in the plush lounge at the Casino Hotel, talking about events of the past. Outside, the sun shone brightly, and I remember gazing abstractly out of the seaward-facing windows. Douglas Bay was the picture of tranquillity, with the sunlight shimmering on the calm blue waters. The promenade was almost deserted – the crowds had thronged to the circuit to witness the spectacle of yet another TT race leaving the streets quiet and empty. Nieto looked at his watch, stood up and said that it was time to go. We shook hands, and the cheerful little Japanese mechanic suddenly looked very sad. He sighed and said, 'My memories of Bill are very good, nice memories.' He grinned ruefully, bade fare-well once more and walked out into the early morning sunshine. There was work to do, more machines to be attended to, other riders to look after . . . but it was obvious that Nieto's thoughts often dwelled in the past. The memories of the days when he worked with the long-haired, fun-loving little Englishman were cherished – never to be forgotten.

9

Indecision

THE FEUD HAD A tremendous effect on Bill, and race organisers found him more difficult as he became touchy, temperamental and totally unpredictable. By the time the rivalry had reached its Monza climax he was in quite a state, emotionally, the final straw being Phil's plan to protest if he hadn't won, which angered and upset Bill more than anything.

All along he had been disgusted by Phil's actions, but the whole affair had no real significance until the final outcome in Italy. Then, to Bill, it seemed as if there was no justice, for bad had triumphed over good, and disloyalty over loyalty. After he lost the title he became incredibly mixed-up. He was disillusioned, bitter, resentful and completely undecided about his future. He began to lose faith in racing and the people connected with it, and he was unsure of who he could trust and who he couldn't. But the thing that hurt him most of all was the attitude of the Press and the public. In their eyes, Phil Read had been forgiven for violating team orders, and had become more popular through winning the 250 championship, while Bill, who hadn't done anything wrong, seemed to be getting all the criticism (mainly over the protest issue), and as a result had lost some of his own popularity. He couldn't understand it at all; hadn't people any sense of values or principles?

No longer did the little figure bounce on to the scene, carefree and happy. The image had gone, and in its place stood a dejected young man, confused and uncertain of what to do next. The smiling jocular air had been replaced by a sombre, quiet manner that seemed strangely out of character.

One week after Monza, at Mallory Park, Bill told *Motor Cycle*, 'I'm fed up with everything and everybody.' And commenting on his protest, he said, 'I had nothing to lose. Before the race, Read said that if I won he would protest about my being under the FIM

minimum weight of 9 stone 6 pounds. If people say it's bad
sportsmanship, that's all right with me – I'm a bad sportsman.
Being a good one didn't do me any good.'

Phil Read was quoted as saying: 'I'm shattered. I can't imagine
anyone making such an obviously transparent protest.'

Immediately after Mallory, where he had fallen yet again on a
damp track when lying second to Mike Hailwood, Bill said that he
was going to fly out to Italy, and would probably stay out of
England for at least a year, returning only to contest his final
meeting at Brands Hatch.

What a final meeting it turned out to be. Brands, the scene of his
début nine years previously, was the venue of Ivy's swansong on
the mighty four-cylinder Yamahas. In front of his home crowd,
Bill won the 125 race by a machine's length from Phil, and both
sliced almost 7 seconds off the lap record. Then, in the closing race
of the day, the two riders lined-up together for the last time on the
powerful Japanese 250s. This was to be the closing chapter . . . the
grand finale.

The pair battled inches apart for the whole ten laps, thrilling the
crowd with their skill and determination. The high-pitched note of
the screaming Yamahas echoed around the Kentish circuit for the
last time as the two super-stars fought for supremacy. Whining
through the nine-speed gearboxes, heeling over into the bends and
hurtling down the straights, the two aces were inseparable. Eight
exhaust pipes merged into a glorious symphony of crescendos,
which rose and fell in unison between one corner and the next,
as the hushed crowd waited expectantly, standing on tiptoe and
squinting as they peered into the gathering dusk to see who would
be leading into the final bend. As the two riders appeared out of
Stirling's Bend and sped towards Clearways it was Phil Read in
front, and he held the advantage to win by a whisker, slicing 1·8
seconds off the lap record in the process. But honours were even.

After the race, Bill shook everyone rigid by announcing his
retirement. The following week's issue of *Motor Cycle News*
carried the front-page headlines, 'IVY QUITS RACING' and Bill
was quoted as saying: 'I'm just too sensitive to put up with all the
bickering and back-biting. I want to get right away from racing . . .
and that includes car events. Not even an offer from Yamaha for
next season would change my mind. I could have ridden one of
Tom Kirby's machines at the last meeting of the season at Brands
Hatch, but I'm not even interested in that. I now realise that I was
never happier than when I was working as a mechanic before I

started racing. The only thing I am thankful for is that I am still alive. There have been times when I thought racing would leave me before I left racing!' Asked about his plans for the future, Bill said that he intended to go into business and planned to open a fashion boutique.

The above statements indicate clearly Ivy's confusion and depression at that time. The very thing for which he had lived and strived so hard to be successful now seemingly meant absolutely nothing to him; he had lost faith in the whole scene. As far as he was concerned, the sportsmanship had gone right out of it, and if the game wasn't to be played to a sporting code and in a happy atmosphere, then it became futile and meaningless.

Various people tried to talk Bill round, and some told him to think about it seriously before making any rash decisions. Others advised him to think it out for the right reasons, and if he still felt that he wanted to call it a day, to retire because he really wanted to, not because of what had happened between him and Phil Read. But all the goodwill and every scrap of advice, although based on the kindest of intentions, did nothing to straighten Bill out, and he remained disheartened and bewildered. Tom Kirby and Chris Lowe gave him the best advice. Their remedy was simple; they told Bill to go abroad for a long break, away from everything, and make his decision after he'd had a good rest. Realising the sense in this, Bill had every intention of doing so, but shortly before he was due to leave for Finland he pranged his Maserati. The accident was not his fault, but his beautiful car was severely dented, which did nothing to cheer him up. He cancelled his holiday plans immediately and rushed around trying to get the car repaired.

It wasn't only the racing which had gone wrong for Bill. Penny Allen, the girl he had been courting for almost a year, had kindly but firmly refused his proposal of marriage. She was the girl, the only girl, with whom Bill ever really fell in love, and he dearly wanted her to marry him. But Penny, although very fond of Bill, had made up her mind that he was not the man she wanted to settle down with, and at her suggestion they broke up and went their separate ways, although Bill felt really lost without her.

It seemed as though Bill really *had* made up his mind to quit. Several weeks after his last race, he said, 'I have not changed my mind, and I don't think there is any likelihood of my doing so.' Commenting on the feud he declared, 'I could stand it for a certain time, but finally it got too much for me. For every person who had

I

something to say for me – there were ten against.' He told Chisholms' that he could have put up with the criticism in the Press, and
he could have put up with Phil Read, 'But I can't put up with
both,' he added.

Throughout the Winter, the Ivy will-he-won't-he-saga continued. Many people thought that he had really retired, but in the
majority were those who knew that racing is in the blood. They
were of the opinion that Ivy's threat to quit was made in a moment
of anger, and that he would be back. Fans wrote to Bill and to the
Press, urging him to think again, expressing their sympathy over
his lost title, and saying that racing just wouldn't be the same
without him.

Rumours still flew round about Yamaha until January 1969
when they announced officially that they would not continue to
run a works team, and told both Ivy and Read that their services
were no longer required. Although it was not released publicly,
Yamaha's planned to return to racing in 1970, and they told Tom
Kirby when he visited Japan that Bill Ivy was the only rider they
wanted. It is interesting to note that they did come back in 1970,
only on a much smaller scale; and that Phil Read, who was one of
the best riders available, was not selected for the team.

Bill was in such a state at this time that he even got on Mike
Hailwood's back at times. But as time wore on and pushed the
unpleasant events further into the past, he began to straighten
himself out again. He was still unhappy and demoralised, but he
began to think constructively about his future, and although he
considered doing lots of things his thoughts always returned to
racing. He was the first to admit that he hadn't much of a head for
business – but what else could he do? After becoming a celebrity,
and used to a high standard of living, the limelight, and the good
money, he couldn't possibly consider drifting back to the obscurity
of working as a mechanic, and the idea of running his own garage
didn't appeal to him. Already he missed doing something, being
someone, and being successful. Racing was his life, and deep-
down he knew that he could never be happy doing anything else.
At the back of his mind, Bill knew that he would take up motor
racing one day, and as the attraction of motorcycles diminished, so
the world of four wheels beckoned and lured him on. The more he
thought about it, the more he was convinced that it was the right
time to make the switch.

As soon as Bill had made up his mind he went straight out and
discussed his plans with various people in the car world, and

having decided to go straight into Formula 2, he bought an ex-works F2 Brabham BT 23C.

'I have had no second thoughts on returning to bike racing since I said I was packing up,' said Bill, 'but I have changed my mind about opening a boutique – motor racing should prove more exciting. I owe everything I have to bikes and the people who support them, but now that Yamaha have pulled out their works team there's nothing left and I wouldn't have a good bike to ride anyway. Even Mike Hailwood is without a ride, so what chance have I got?'

The news of Ivy's decision to take up motor racing had hardly been in print when fresh rumours and speculation swept through the racing world. Ivy's name was being linked with Jawa, the Czechoslovakian motorcycle concern, who had brought out a new 350cc four-cylinder two-stroke racing motorcycle. Although he denied that he was interested in riding the machine, Bill admitted that he had written to the Jawa people. 'But that was a long time ago,' he said, 'it's just talk. Anyway, they couldn't afford me and from now on I'm a motor racing driver. It's extremely unlikely that I'll ever compete on bikes again. As yet, I haven't even sat in my car, but everything should be ready for competition in March. I'm just going to give it a try and see how things go.'

Even away from the racing scene, Bill still managed to get himself into some awkward situations. At Christmas he was tramping on through the deserted London suburbs in his Maserati when a police car stopped him at a set of traffic lights. Bill was told to get out of his car, and one of the policemen challenged, 'You must be drunk to drive like that!'

And Bill *had* been drinking, not excessively, but he certainly didn't want a breathalyser test because he'd had two or three Bacardi and cokes. 'Drunk?', he said, 'I'm not drunk. Look, I'll prove to you that I'm not even tipsy.' And before an audience of two astonished policemen, Bill walked up and down the pavement – on his hands! Whether it was the spirit of Christmas, or whether it was the strange circumstances which appealed to the policemen's sense of humour, who can say? Anyway, Bill's performance convinced the coppers that he was fit enough to drive, and he escaped with a caution.

Then, just as Bill was beginning to feel more like his old self again, a terrible tragedy hit the Ivy family. Mr Ivy, who had been in hospital since suffering a stroke at Brands Hatch, died in mid-January. Bill was tremendously cut-up about it, and he moved back to his mother's home for a while where he would sometimes sit alone in his room for hours. For a long time he never even bothered to go out, but he was marvellous to his mum in the way he looked after, comforted and did all he could for her.

Losing his father came as a bitter shock to Bill, and he missed his dad terribly. After the funeral, some of the people who had attended went back to the Ivys' home for refreshments, as is customary, but poor Bill just couldn't understand this at all. 'Why?' he asked his mother. 'This is a funeral not a wedding! Anyone would think we're celebrating instead of mourning . . . why don't they all go away and leave us alone?' Mrs Ivy tried to explain, but he wouldn't listen and shut himself in his room until everybody had left. Sad and confused, all Bill understood was that 'Ringo' had gone, and he would never see him again.

It was several weeks before he began to cheer up again, and even then there were times when he lapsed into dismal silence. He was very concerned about his mother, too. 'You will be very lonely now dad's gone,' he told her, 'and when the racing season starts again I'll be away most of the time and you'll be all alone in the house. You must find an interest – something to do to take your mind off things.'

The rumours linking Ivy and Jawa grew, and in early February Bill disclosed that he had been in contact with the Czech factory, and that he had been invited to Prague for talks. He was obviously reluctant to say anything to the Press after his previous claim to have abandoned motorcycle racing for good. He had wanted to try the Jawa without anyone knowing, and then, if he considered the machine to be good enough, to announce publicly that he intended to race it. But somehow the news leaked out, so Bill had no choice but to reveal his plans.

He flew out to Czechoslovakia, was shown over the Jawa factory and had a good look at the new bike. A test outing was laid on, and Franta Stastny, the ever-cheerful Czech veteran, told Bill that the experimental V4 engine had seized countless times in previous test runs, and that there was a good chance of it seizing again as the problem had not been eliminated. 'So what?' Bill had said. 'The Yamahas seized as well – come on, let's get on with it!' Franta was amazed. He really thought that Ivy would decline to even test ride the machine until it had been virtually sorted-out, and he admired the little Englishman's courage. After that he always referred to Bill as 'the leetle man with the beeg heart'.

Ivy was so impressed with the Jawa's potential that he agreed immediately to race it in all the world championship rounds, with the exception of the TT. Understandably, he wasn't keen on the idea of racing an undeveloped, seizure-prone machine in the Isle of Man, but he stated that if the TT was vital to their championship chances, then he would compete there as well.

'They are tremendously keen,' Bill told his mother on his return to England, 'and if only you could see what they are trying to do on such a limited budget. They have none of the vast resources that Yamaha have. In comparison, Jawa are really having a go on a shoe-string, but the bike is fantastic, and when it's developed I reckon it'll be a winner.'

The news of Ivy's return to motorcycle racing cheered enthusiasts everywhere, for with Mike Hailwood finally retiring from bikes to concentrate on cars, and the withdrawal of all the Japanese works teams, the grand prix scene looked very bleak. Consequently, the anticipated threat to Giacomo Agostini's monopoly of the 350cc world championship on the MV was very welcome, and everybody looked forward to seeing Ivy challenge the Italian on Czechoslovakia's most powerful motorcycle.

The main reason for Ivy's return to motorcycles was money. He intended to go into motor racing on a make-or-break system, and he needed the money from his Jawa contract to help subsidise the enormous costs involved in his car-racing début. 'The cash I earn from bikes will be my bread and butter,' Bill told his mother. He planned to mix the two sports, which would involve a hectic schedule, until he established himself on four wheels.

Competing seriously in both spheres of racing is an almost impossible task, as Mike Hailwood discovered when he tried to combine motor and motorcycle racing. But Bill had made up his mind to give it a fair try, and he intended to compete in as many Formula 2 championship events as he could, in between his 350cc grand prix motorcycle commitments. This meant dashing from one country to another and often driving thousands of miles at top speed in an effort to reach the next venue in time. To overcome this problem, Bill decided to buy an aeroplane, but when he told his mother that he had placed an order for one she became very worried. 'Oh Bill,' she said, 'you're really over-stepping yourself – you'll never be able to afford to run the car *and* a plane!'

'But I shan't keep the car,' he explained, 'and I can nearly buy a plane for what I can get for the Maserati. Then, when I fly to places I can hire a car when I get there. It will be so much cheaper, and quicker too. All the others who travel by plane have told me this.'

However, Mrs Ivy was still worried, for she knew it would cost Bill virtually everything he had to try to establish himself in the highly competitive world of motor racing. 'You watch you don't bankrupt yourself,' she told him with typical motherly concern. 'If it gets to the stage where you find you're running short, you can sell the bungalow and have that money, and I'll find a smaller place to live.'

Bill was horrified at this suggestion. 'What! Sell the bungalow?' he replied indignantly. 'For goodness sake, that's *your* home. If things get that bad I'll sell the flat and move back home.'

10

Motor racing and Jawa

IVY FIRST TRIED the Brabham at Goodwood, and promptly lapped within 3 seconds of the Formula 2 lap record. Nobby Clark, Mike Hailwood's mechanic and a close friend, went with him, and while Bill was out on the circuit a spectator ambled over and started chatting. 'I don't know who the guy was,' recounts Nobby, 'but he said that he had never seen anyone go as quickly as Bill on their first time out, and he reckoned he'd seen quite a few.'

At Oulton Park the following week Ivy spun due to over-confidence. He accelerated too hard out of Cascades (a tricky downhill left-hander), and ran off the circuit on to the infield. Completely out of control, the car then hit a bank, which deflected it right across the track into the rough on the opposite side, where it finally came to a standstill. Bill was unhurt, but the Brabham looked very secondhand. However, a thorough stripdown revealed the damage to be only superficial, and undaunted, Bill set about preparing the car for his début at Thruxton on Easter Monday.

When Ivy first discussed his motor racing plans with Harry Downing, of BP, Harry had said, 'Well, you will obviously start in Formula Ford or Formula 3, Bill?' He had the shock of his life when Bill calmly said that he intended to go straight into Formula 2!

'I couldn't understand this at all,' said Harry, 'because most people who drive in Formula 2 have worked their way up to it, and for a man to switch from two wheels to four, and to go directly into Formula 2 is like pitching yourself in the deep end if you can't swim. It involves laying out a hell of a lot of money, and either you're a success or a complete and utter failure. Quite frankly, when Bill told me that he had settled for F2 I didn't think he would make the grade because it is so competitive, and the drivers are men who have raced on four wheels for a number of years, and already established themselves in the lower grades. To go straight in against such experienced opposition ... well, I said to him, "You must be mad, Bill", but he replied, *"I'm going to do F2 or nothing!"*

'I had seen Bill perform in a Formula Ford some years previously, and I knew that he had a lot of potential, but it wasn't until Thruxton on his first F2 outing that I realised just how good he was. After practice we were all chatting in the BP caravan when Bill came dashing in with a practice time sheet, which grades all the drivers for grid positions in the heats. Naturally, the fastest men get the places on the front, but when Bill showed me the sheet I could hardly believe it. "Look, Harry," he said, "I've got pole position on the grid – *in front of Jackie Stewart!* ... But I'm going to ask the stewards to put me at the back of the grid." I said, "Don't be a bloody clot, Bill." And he said, "But I've never been out on the track before in a Formula 2 race." He was actually worried about getting in the other drivers' way! I told him not to worry, and advised him to stop a couple of times on his warming-up lap to practise starting.

'Prior to the start I spoke to Jochen Rindt, Graham Hill and Piers Courage, and asked them what they thought of little Bill as a driver. All three said that he was fantastic, and definitely had a tremendous amount of potential. Everyone was amazed, because it was so unusual for a man to go from two wheels to four and to go so quickly so soon. Of all the British motorcyclists who have had a crack at motor racing, only John Surtees and Mike Hailwood have been really successful, but Ivy's début, in comparison ... well, everybody was saying that he was a natural.

'During the heat, I shall always remember, the commentator was wildly enthusiastic about Bill. He said, *"This man Ivy is fantastic – his lines are so precise."* For an announcer to say this at a Formula 2 meeting was so unusual, and personally I have never heard anybody spoken about with so much enthusiasm. He said, "Surely this man must be spotted and taken up by somebody."

'At Thruxton, Bill more than justified himself, and I was so mortified after doubting his ability – he absolutely shattered me.'

No wonder the car world was so impressed. Ivy finished fourth in his heat, behind Stewart, Jean-Pierre Beltoise, and Hill, and in the final his engine blew up when he was holding a superb fifth. Only Rindt had been faster in practice, and Ivy had set an equal time with Stewart, in front of such stars as Beltoise, Hill, Courage, and Clay Regazzoni.

After the races, Bill asked his mother if he looked steady. She told him that he looked fine, adding, 'But it frightened the life out of me just watching you tear round like that.' He replied, 'Huh, frightened *you*? . . . It scared the *life* out of me!'

At Thruxton, Bill was invited to the commentator's box to be interviewed, and the first question the announcer asked him was, 'You only look about 14 – how old are you?' 'Fourteen!' Bill replied with his characteristic wit.

After all his upsets in the bike world, losing his father, and breaking-up with Penny, everything seemed to be going fine once more. He enjoyed the new challenge of motor racing, he was pleased with his initial outing at Thruxton, and he liked the people in the car world. But most of all, he was delighted because he and Penny had gone back together again – that meant more to him than anything.

'Before we broke up,' explained Penny, 'Billy asked me to marry him, but I didn't want to get married. I didn't think he was the right man for me, and I was making him very unhappy. My mother gave me a good talking to and said, "Look, either you want him or you don't want him. He's a nice boy, and I'm very, very fond of him – I don't think it's fair." When you reach a certain stage in a relationship, you either make it or break it, and I thought it was best to break it.

'I was convinced that Billy wasn't the right one for me. He wasn't the sort of man I'd been used to. He was younger, rather naïve and not very worldly. I'd been with older, more sophisticated people, and he was completely the opposite of everything I'd been used to, and the more I would tell myself this, the more keen he was getting, or so it seemed. It was only after we broke up and I wasn't with him that I realised how stupid these superficial things are – it's the person underneath that matters. I went back to the sophisticated people and all that . . . and I wasn't happy.

'Although I don't like to admit it, I did give him a bit of a hard time. I always knew exactly what he thought of me, which was very nice, but at the time I think I probably took advantage of it. It was only through being on my own for a while that I realised I had been very silly, and that he *was* the right boy for me, that I did want to marry him, and that I was a very lucky girl.

'But everybody makes mistakes; any two people have their troubles in courtship, and ours weren't any different from anybody else's. We went back together and I was very happy, and I think he was. We would probably have got married fairly quickly; certainly not that Summer, because Billy was racing, there was so much to do, and I wasn't in England anyway, but I think we would have after the Summer. When you have been with somebody, and you've had a lot of ups and downs, when you do get back together and you're settled there's not much point in putting it off. You both know what you want, you're happy together, and Billy wanted children.'

It took a lot of cash to repair the Cosworth engine after its Thruxton blow-up, for the damage was quite extensive. Bill had the car prepared and he travelled down to Pau, in France, in the hope of better luck. But again he was forced to pull out of the race, this time with a jammed throttle. He fared no better at Nurburgring in West Germany, either, for after being second-fastest in training he had a colossal accident at around 130 mph in the race. Miraculously, he emerged unscathed, and in that respect he was lucky, but he still hadn't finished a race. Despite this, he was beginning to make his mark in motor racing, and people were predicting that he was a star of the future. Some even went so far as to say that he showed all the promise of a potential world champion. Here, Jackie Stewart talks about Bill:

'I think the thing that most impressed me about Billy was his tremendous personality. In my experience, I don't think there has been anyone in motor racing quite like Bill Ivy.

'To begin with, he came into motor racing in a way we all heard about. We heard there was this motorcyclist who was going to come motor racing, and his name was Bill Ivy. I heard from a friend in a clothing shop in London that some guy called Bill Ivy had been in with Mike Hailwood to buy clothes, and this was the first time I heard his name mentioned. I had never seen him, but I took particular note of his motorcycling successes. Then I heard that he had bought Jochen Rindt's old Brabham, that he'd been to Oulton Park practising, and that he'd been having a pretty heroic time. Then, finally, I met him one night in the "Revolution" discotheque in London . . . and there was Billy with some very attractive young lady. He was smaller than me, so that was a change, and I suppose because of that I sort of took to him in a way.

'Then, when the motor racing season started, Billy came in. And here was this chap with the hipster trousers, with a skinny-knit sweater that never really met his trousers, hair much longer than mine, and sort of . . . very quick on his feet and rather cocky in a way, I felt sure, a lot of people were going to be put off. It wasn't a case of motor racing thinking the wrong way – I mean, motor racing is very, very democratic nowadays – but here was Billy, who was a kind of new concept to everybody, and I thought, "Well, he's going to have trouble." But he came in with such a remarkable personality that everybody who came in contact with him immediately took to him.

'The people one would have expected to like him – because he was a very likeable man – *did* like him; but the people one would expect to be reserved and remote towards him, were remote towards him only until they got to know him just a little bit, then he completely won them over, in fact they became his biggest fans. They were the people who supported him more and really spoke more for him than anybody else.

'He used to come round and talk Formula 2 with me – gear ratios, etc – and he was tremendously enthusiastic about his driving, hoping that it was going to mean something for him in the future. He had tremendous talent, and *more natural ability than anyone I had seen coming into motor racing*.

'He was going through the initial stage of motor racing. Surtees went through it, other motorcyclists who have gone over to cars have been through it, and Gary Hocking was going through it and he lost his life while doing so – but I felt that Billy had more natural talent. He went round the Nurburgring, the first time he had ever been there in a car, and I think he was second or third fastest in the rain, or on a damp track anyway, and this was something very outstanding for me. I thought he was a tremendous driver, and if life had allowed him the opportunity of proving himself, once he had gone through the settling-down stage I'm sure he would have been a big name – without doubt. Not only a big name through his talent, but also a great favourite through his flamboyant personality.

'In his first Formula 2 meeting at Thruxton we had an equal time during practice, but because Billy had set-up his time earlier in the session, he earned pole position for the heat.

'One of my happiest memories of Billy was at the Nurburgring races in April 1969. I won the race and Billy had an enormous accident on one of the fastest and most dangerous parts of the circuit – it had knocked all the wheels off and done a really big job on his car – and afterwards we all went to the prizegiving at the Sports Hotel. The presentation of prizes was taking place, the officials on the top table were all very smartly dressed in their blazers and what-have-you, and we were all on one very large table

at the side. In the middle of all this, the president happened to get
up out of his seat and went off to do something, and Billy sat down
in *his* seat! Of course to begin with nobody at the table wanted anything to do with this long-haired, skinny-knit-low-cut-trouser-guy,
until all of a sudden he had them eating out of his hand, was drinking their wine, and passing their wine underneath the table to his
mechanic, who was crawling along and supplying it to our table,
and of course we were in stitches. That night Billy got pretty
happy. . . .'

Coming from a world champion, Jackie Stewart's remarks about
a man who had only just entered the sport are praise indeed, and
another champion, Graham Hill, virtually echoed Jackie's comments:

'The thing that amazed me was the way Bill Ivy came into
motor racing,' said Graham. 'It wasn't a gradual process, he just
arrived, and bang – there he was. And right from the start his
ability was beyond question. At his first Formula 2 meeting he
made an incredible lap time during practice – extremely fast – and
he followed this up everywhere he appeared by going very quickly
and getting up to the front among the leading drivers. I thought he
showed remarkable talent by such a rapid adaptation to motor
racing after stepping across from motorcycling, because it doesn't
always follow that just because a person is good at one, they will
be any good at the other. All the attributes are common in both
sports, but the technique is vastly different from riding a bike to
driving a car. One is leaning over, and the other is sliding, and of
course they demand completely different techniques, but Bill
adapted himself immediately and showed tremendous flair. I mean
he would go quickly, *very* quickly.

'Yet he had no side to him, and he certainly didn't push himself
on anybody; he didn't come into motor racing giving anyone the
impression that he was a world champion in another sphere. He
wasn't swollen-headed or anything, in fact he was only too ready to
learn, and he didn't seem to have any problem about asking questions. Often he would come over and consult me about something,
and I was only too pleased to oblige by helping him if I could. I
think he was slightly surprised that he was doing so well – so was I!
Most of the motorcyclists who turn to motor racing do reasonably
well, but Bill was outstanding, and to learn so quickly was a
tremendous achievement.

'Another thing was his size. He was so small he must have been a designer's dream, because to be able to design a car small enough to fit him, you could *really* have a small car. If you've got to make them to fit myself, or Dan Gurney, then you've got to make a much larger car – then you've got a bigger frontal area so there's more wind-drag, and more weight. Apart from that, Bill weighed 50 pounds less than me, and a designer will spend a fortune trying to produce a car just 20 pounds lighter, so you can imagine the advantages of such a small driver. He really *was* a designer's dream, and undoubtedly he would have got into a works team with no problem at all.

'Bill was a very likeable person, too, and he had a humorous and very ready wit, with quick replies. His was a cockney-style humour, and I must say that I appreciate cockney humour – I think it's some of the funniest in the world, and he had an abundance of it.

'I remember the party we had at the Sport Hotel after the Nurburgring races in Germany. It was very amusing and Bill was in tremendous form and had us in fits of laughter. I won't say that all the German officials approved of his antics at the prizegiving; at first they were more than a little taken aback, but he soon won them over. Then he danced with Francis Cevert's tall blonde girlfriend and, well . . . his eyes just about came level with her boobs! There he was, dancing with this enormous girl who was very well endowed, with his face well and truly planted between her charlies. Of course, this had everyone in stitches. It was really amusing, and she took it very well – actually, she probably enjoyed it. Bill left an impression on everybody!'

Although Bill had presented a picture of gaiety at the Sport Hotel that evening, few people would have guessed that underneath that exterior he was feeling far from happy. When the party broke up and everyone went to bed he felt most deflated, so he got in his car and drove all the way to the coast, caught the night boat and arrived back in England early the following morning. Mrs Ivy was amazed to see him back so soon. He told her that he had driven all through the night, and that he felt fed-up. 'What happened? I see from the papers that your car was badly damaged,' she said. 'Yes,' he told her, 'but it's not as bad as I thought at first.' Then he spoke in a way that his mother had never known before. Whether he had experienced the first feelings of an impending doom, prior to his dreadful premonition, or whether it was merely a chance remark, but speaking of his accident he said, 'Do you know, by all the rules I shouldn't be here. You know, *I think me luck's running out, Ethel!*'

In all the years Bill had been racing, Mrs Ivy had never, ever heard him say anything like that.

On his first ride on the Jawa, in Italy, Bill retired with a seized engine, and the same thing happened at the Spanish Grand Prix. But at Hockenheim, in the West German round, it seemed as if the temperamental four-cylinder two-stroke was well on the way to being sorted-out. Although Agostini won the race, Ivy finished a magnificent second, just 20 seconds behind, and Franta Stastny brought the other Jawa home third. These results were encouraging; they were early days yet, but the bikes already were showing a lot of promise, and the Czechoslovakian team increased their efforts on the machines. The Jawas obviously had the right ingredients of speed, handling and braking, but they had been lacking in reliability, although their results in Germany suggested that they had gone part of the way towards finding some.

Whilst Hockenheim was kind to Ivy on the Jawa, it certainly wasn't when he raced the Brabham there, and after being second fastest in practice, he went out of the race with a broken gear selector rod. He was leading at the time, with just five laps to go.

Until 1969, Bill had enjoyed the travelling, but when he mixed both car and bike racing he began to detest it. He found the hectic schedule extremely fatiguing, and he told his mother that the long journeys from one country to another were becoming a chore. Although he had ordered an aeroplane, Bill hadn't qualified for his pilot's licence, so he had no option but to use the car. Mrs Ivy suggested that he could get a pilot to fly him around, but he wouldn't hear of that. For some reason the idea of being flown by someone else didn't appeal to him, and he preferred to travel by car until he got his licence.

After competing in a car meeting at Zolder, in Belgium, where he finished fourth in one heat, spun off in the other, and finished fifth on aggregate, Ivy drove down to Italy for another Formula 2 event. There, after a disagreement with officials, he declined to race and drove straight on to Holland to race the Jawa in the Dutch TT.

Tom Kirby was sitting out on the hotel veranda having a drink when the big red Maserati came roaring down the street towards him. The car pulled up and Bill got out, stiff and weary from his marathon journey across Switzerland, France and Belgium. He told Tom that he had driven all the way, only stopping for petrol. 'What the hell did you do that for?' asked Tom. Bill recounted what had happened. 'I had to keep driving, Uncle,' he said, 'I left the car meeting after I had a row with the ruddy officials – and I had a shunt in practice.' Tom told him not to worry and said that he would fix him up with a room at the hotel so that he could get some rest.

'I shall never forget that evening,' Tom Kirby related. 'Bill and I were having a quiet drink and a chat. He seemed much more subdued than usual, as if he had something on his mind and was brooding on it. Then suddenly he said, "Uncle – *I'm going to crash and get killed this year!*" Just like that, right out of the blue. It really shook me. "Don't talk bloody stupid, you don't want to say things like that," I said. But he went on, "In a car, I'm going to crash . . . this year." He was really serious about it, and I had to be quite firm with him. "Come on," I said, "let's not hear another word about it. Jawa's have been round to see if you've arrived yet, they've got great hopes for you, and the bikes are all ready. You're whacked out. What you need is a really good night's sleep and you'll be all right in the morning."'

After Bill had gone to bed, Tom tried to dismiss the incident from his mind. He tried to tell himself that the reason for Bill's odd behaviour was fatigue, and that he was still annoyed over his row with the officials at Monza. But he couldn't forget those words, for in all the time he had known the little chap, he had never heard him say anything like it. However, Bill never mentioned it again during the rest of his stay in Assen.

Whatever were Ivy's thoughts, they didn't stop him from putting on his usual performance, in fact he excelled himself at Assen and rode the race of his life. He flung the huge Jawa past Agostini's MV during the early stages of the 350cc race, and the 100,000 spectators went wild with excitement. Then the bike faltered, and Bill dropped back as one cylinder cut-out. The crowd groaned in sympathy, for the battle seemed to be over as Agostini roared on to what appeared to be yet another unchallenged victory. But the Jawa suddenly chimed back on all cylinders again, and Ivy started to gain ground. With the fans waving and cheering their encouragement, he set about the impossible task of catching the flying Italian. Every time the riders appeared they were closer together for Ivy was gaining ground at the rate of 100 yards a lap. He swept into the lead on the twelfth lap, and the delighted crowd went mad. Agostini fought gamely, but there was nothing he could do about it, and the diminutive figure, almost dwarfed by the big Jawa, pulled away relentlessly. It seemed as if Bill had the race in his pocket, until the fickle machine began to slow again, and the Italian regained the lead and went on to win – a very lucky man.

Dark, swarthy and good-looking, Giacomo remembers that day in Holland in 1969: 'Bill Ivy was a very good rider,' he said, 'and he gave me a hard ride at Assen, really pushed me. I was trying very hard, and Bill, he was in front of me. If the Jawa had not broken down it would have been very close at the feenish.'

He went on to say, 'Bill was a good friend. Sometimes with him we go to dance, because him, is like me – like the girls and like joking with the girls.' Apparently, they would both try to chat-up each other's admirers, and Giacomo said, 'Yes, but it's not a feex girlfriend. You know, one girl here, another girl another place. We always joking – it was good fun.'

After the Dutch, Bill had a few days' break before his next engagement, so he motored down to Spain for a short holiday, and to see Penny, who was staying in Marbella. Although he still enjoyed mild flirtations with his many female fans, Bill had eyes only for Penny since they had been together again, and he was looking forward very much to seeing her.

'The day before Billy went away for his last trip on the Continent he came to my house,' said Penny. 'I was going to Spain a week later, and he was going to come down to see me between races. We were talking about what we were going to do, and what a lovely Summer we were going to have. We were so peaceful then. . . .'

As Bill was constantly dashing from one country to another, it became very difficult for him and Penny to keep in touch. They would write to Mrs Ivy, in England, enclosing letters to each other, which she would then forward on, making sure in Bill's case that his mail arrived at his next destination in time. The system was a good one, but it caused a considerable delay before the couple received each other's letters. Bill had written to Penny, via his mother, but he had no way of knowing whether his letter would arrive in time to let her know that he was coming.

Unbeknown to Bill, Penny had decided to spend a few days in Portugal with some friends, and she had left Marbella just two days before the letter arrived at her flat in Spain. When Bill got there he found the flat empty, and a pile of unopened letters on the mat. The people who had let the property didn't know where Penny was, and Bill became very worried. He toured all the clubs, restaurants and bars, asking everyone if they had seen a 'blonde English girl called Penny', but nobody had. Then he heard that two girls had been murdered in the vicinity, just before he arrived, and fearing the worst he went to the police, then to the mortuary

John Stoddart's camera caught Bill with
the twin-cylinder 250cc Yamaha at
Brands Hatch and produced one of the
finest action shots ever taken of him.

Above: Bill with Penny Allen, the only girl he wanted to marry. *Left:* The other great love of his life was his Ferrari, which he always referred to as 'a great crumpet-wagon!'

A joke shared by two masters.
Bill in lighthearted mood with the
brilliant Giacomo Agostini.

Bill's switch to four wheels
brought some welcome good
humour to racing car paddocks.
He and Jackie Stewart rib each
other about their long hair before
a Formula 2 race; earlier they
had set identical practice times!

Top: After turning his back on motorcycle racing at the end of 1968, Bill relented and accepted Jawa's invitation to ride their experimental works two-stroke. He rode the machine with characteristic brilliance... *Above:* The Bill Ivy Brabham, carrying the tall front and rear wings permitted early in 1969, holds off Brambilla's Ferrari at the Easter International Formula 2 race at Thruxton.

Bill was in serious mood in the paddock at Sachsenring, and when he lined up for his last practice session … *Below:* The point at which the Jawa left the slippering circuit and fatally injured its gallant rider.

Above: An unknown admirer painted Bill Ivy's name and a cross on a tower near Plauen in East Germany as a tribute. *Right:* Bill's name was perpetuated through the magnificent silver trophy which became a coveted award in motorcycle racing. Mrs Ivy congratulates the 1970 winner Peter Williams.

'Bill's Team'. Mrs Ivy astride the Ivy Yamaha which was presented to her by the Japanese works in Bill's memory, and which became an important part of the racing scene. Behind the machine are Rex Butcher, who rode it until his retirement in 1971, his successor, Jim Harvey, and Tom Kirby, who played such a big part in helping Bill Ivy to stardom.

to look at the bodies. Apparently at this stage they had not been identified, and after performing this unpleasant task, Bill was so relieved to find that he recognised neither one. But where had Penny gone? He had phoned her parents and his mother, but they hadn't heard from her for over a week, and presumed that she was still at the same address. It was all very worrying, but Bill told himself that it was no good fearing the worst, and that there was probably a simple explanation for Penny's disappearance. He tried to stop thinking about it and decided to look up Lady Sarah Courage, who was on holiday somewhere between Marbella and Estepona.

When the material for this book was being gathered during 1970, a list was compiled of people who could have contributed reminiscences and opinions of Bill and his career. It was intended to interview every one of them, but tragically, Piers Courage was involved in a terrible fatal accident that year in the Dutch Grand Prix at Zandvoort. The need to talk to Lady Sarah about Bill's last days so soon after her own great loss was extremely unfortunate, but she had to be approached because she was the last person to see Bill before he travelled down to East Germany. Revealing courage by nature as well as by name, Lady Sarah (Sally to her friends) insisted on helping all she could, and has provided a vital link in the final chapter of this biography. Without this contribution by a charming, beautiful lady the story would have been incomplete. Here it is in her own words:

'Piers and Bill had often spent a lot of amusing times together, but the first time I really got to know him was at Zolder. Billy was there with his lovely car, absolutely flashing about trying to pick up all the birds!

'He was such fun, and absolutely mad as a hatter. He was such fun to be with, so cheeky and nice, and appearing to be sort of . . . irresponsible. He would go round calling his mechanic "My man". He always used to call him that. Suddenly he would put on a great 'plummy' voice and say, "My man – my man will see to it", or "My man, do that", and in mock exasperation, "My man, you've done it absolutely *all* wrong!" It was marvellous. He never seemed to bother that much, and yet he went so well. If his car went wrong he would say, "Oh well, blown-up today – can't be bothered, you know – shan't go out, then." You never heard him moaning, and that was amazing. A lot of the drivers come up with stories and whine over why they didn't go fast enough – because this wasn't

K

right, or the car wasn't good enough, or something – but I never heard Billy make an excuse. My father always said that a good racing driver never blames his car, unless it's obviously at fault; then he should find out why the machinery isn't going properly, not broadcast and whine it abroad as an excuse. Even if his car gave trouble, Billy never moaned. He always laughed and said, "Oh well, I didn't do it right."

'I don't know much about people choosing drivers, but everybody was saying that Billy was the man to get because he was going to be tops. You'd hear people saying, "Gosh, we must get Bill Ivy in our team for next year."

'I was sitting in his Maserati at Zolder, and he said, "I think I'll go for a drive round the circuit – no need to get out, I'll go very slowly." Ohhh ... three laps later! I was sitting there trying to play it very cool, but after a while I put the safety belt on and just sat there with my eyes closed. We were hurtling round at very high speed – and he was only going round to learn the circuit! He was making comments the whole time. "I don't know how they do this one. ... Don't think I'm going to do this right. ... No, that's not quite how they do it. ... I know, I shall follow somebody!" Then he must have noticed that I had my eyes tight shut, and he asked me if I was frightened. "No, no, Billy," I said, "it's lovely I've never done anything like this in my life before ... don't think I'd like to do it again ... can we go in now?!!"

'Again at Zolder, we were fooling around, I and another girl, and Billy said, "'Ere, hold my helmet." I was just sort of idling away the time with nothing to do, and I had some of those felt pens, so I started tracing out ivy leaves all over the helmet. Then we drew stars and stripes in red and blue, and terrible things, well, silly sort of sayings like, "I like pot", and "Ivy leaves town." It looked absolutely shocking – and he actually raced in it. He didn't even bother to wipe it off! I was so embarrassed, because he kept going round saying, "She's done it!" I wished I'd never been given those wretched felt pens!

'When Billy said that he was going to Spain the same time as we were, I said, "Come and visit us." Before we left England I gave his mother the telephone number of the villa we had booked. I don't know what happened, but I think I must have got the number wrong, because he spent a whole week going flat-out up and down between Marbella and Estepona on the Costa Del Sol, trying to find these extraordinary people! And I don't think he ever forgave us; he spent so much on petrol he could have killed us all!

'He found us, eventually, and we said, "Well, what have you been doing?" And he said, "Well, I'm working, actually." He told us that he was working as a barman for 15 bob a day! He had decided that he would work in this bar in the evenings for 15 bob! He did *absolutely* no work at all, didn't know how to pour out a drink, and gave everybody *great* big drinks. I should think they lost so much money, because I'm sure that he should have measured out thimblefuls like they do in English pubs.

'And he thoroughly disrupted the life of these rather nice villas with crowds of English people in them. All these people lying out there, looking like lobsters and thinking they looked so marvellous, with this amazing little character with long hair shouting out to them, "'Ullo missis – 'ere, you're going pink!", and they just couldn't take it. He was the most wonderful company. I think he made us laugh more in three days than one usually laughs in six months. It was fantastic, and we had a lovely time. He was with us every day for these three days, playing around, and shark fishing out in a boat (which absolutely terrified me out of my life!).

'I only knew him for a short time, although I'd heard so much about him, but Piers and I thought he was one of the *greatest* people we had ever met. Really, both of us only knew him for such a short time, yet he and Piers seemed to click and laugh at exactly the same things. They would talk for hours, and I remember one lunchtime at Zolder we were nearly late for practice because both of them were "rabbitting" on so much. They got on so well, which was super, and they laughed at the same sort of things, which was so nice. Perhaps one wouldn't have thought those two would have done, because they were entirely different people, but they did. I think Piers and I were so lucky to have known Billy; even if it was only for a little while it was worth it, it really was.

'He was so devoted to his family, and absolutely amazing to his mother. He was always talking about her, worrying about her, and wondering if she was all right. It was *so* nice to hear somebody really adoring their mother, and talking about his sisters and every-thing. He often talked about them, and what he was going to do, and about racing. He really thought he might give up bike racing altogether, even before he got sponsored in Formula 2, but he said that it was his bread and butter.

'It was awful, because he said to me the day before he left for East Germany, "I really don't want to go this weekend, I really don't." And I said, "Then *don't* go, Billy. If you really feel that you're not happy about going – in your mind – just don't go." He told me that he had to. "Sally, I've got to," he said, "it is my bread and butter, you know – I *must* go." I tried to persuade him not to. "Well, it's up to you," I said, "but if you feel uneasy about it, I personally wouldn't go." But it was no good; although he was very reluctant about going he said that he couldn't let the motorcycle people down, so off he went. It was the last time we ever saw him!'

Bill arrived at Sachsenring the day before practice, and immediately contacted England for news of Penny. He was very relieved to learn that she was perfectly all right, and had left a message asking him to ring her as soon as he could. Straight-away he booked a long-distance call to Portugal and succeeded in obtaining the right number, only to learn that Penny was spending the day on the beach. After trying again later in the afternoon, Bill finally got through that evening. 'As long as you're all right . . . I've been so worried about you,' he told her. For a whole hour they chatted away – there was so much to talk about because they hadn't seen each other for so long.

In his telephone conversation with Penny, Bill had sounded quite normal and cheerful, and he mentioned nothing of his reluctance about competing in the forthcoming race. However, the few people who had dinner with Bill later in the evening noticed that the little chap wasn't his usual buoyant self. In fact he hardly spoke or smiled at all, and of all the photographs that were taken of him at Sachsenring there is not one in which he looks happy; he appears to be in a sombre, serious mood in every picture.

The speculation and excitement surrounding the anticipated battle between Ivy and Agostini began to grow, even before practice started. Many thousands of fans swarmed to the circuit, braving the wet, dismal conditions just to watch the training sessions. By race day the crowd was expected to swell to 150,000.

Bill warmed-up the Jawa and went out on to the track for his first practice stint. He hadn't even got down to lapping seriously, and by his own standards was virtually touring, cautiously testing the treacherous conditions. Then, rounding a long, fast left-hander, the Jawa's engine seized solid and Bill crashed heavily into a wall which was not protected by straw bales. He suffered severe head and chest injuries, and was rushed to Leichtenstein hospital, near Karl-Marx-Stadt, where he was placed in an oxygen tent in a bid to save his life.

While the news of Bill's accident was relayed to broadcasting systems throughout the world, Mrs Ivy busied herself with the housework, not knowing that her son was seriously injured and fighting for his life. It was Sue, Bill's elder sister, who first heard the news and dashed down the road to tell her mother. Nobody had contacted Mrs Ivy, and she knew no more about Bill than the millions who had heard the radio bulletin.

Together, Sue and her mother waited anxiously for the next newsflash. Then it came over: 'Bill Ivy, Britain's motorcycle ace, was rushed to hospital seriously injured after falling from his machine this morning. . . .' A few moments later the phone rang. It was Geoff Clarke, chief of the motor racing school at Brands Hatch. He had only just heard about Bill, and he immediately phoned Mrs Ivy to make all the necessary arrangements to fly her out to East Germany as quickly as possible. 'Keep this line open,' said Geoff, 'and I'll ring you back as soon as I can.' While he was in the middle of contacting the German Embassy an announcement came over the television stating that Bill Ivy had died. In her anxiety, Mrs Ivy had forgotten to switch on her television; she had been listening to the radio for further news. Consequently, when Geoff phoned back, he had the unpleasant task of breaking the news to her.

At Sachsenring, the awful tragedy plunged the whole scene into an atmosphere of gloom. Leslie Nichol, the *Daily Express* reporter, wrote: 'The news stunned the whole paddock. I saw riders, noted for their daring and toughness, break down in tears.'

One eye-witness said that Ivy had taken his left hand off the handlebar to adjust the position of his helmet or goggles, and at that precise moment the bike had seized-up on the lower left-hand cylinder. If this was the case – and there is some confusion about what actually did happen because hardly anyone saw the accident – then Bill never stood a chance. If he had his left hand off the bars he would never have reached the clutch in time to release the drive to the back wheel. The clutch is the two-stroke rider's life-line, and if it is not released the instant the engine seizes, then the rear wheel locks up, throwing the machine into a vicious, uncontrollable skid. An experienced rider such as Bill would hardly fail to grab the clutch in time if he had his left hand in its usual position.

During the crash Ivy's helmet came off, but why it should have done remains a complete mystery. One theory is that he had not fastened the helmet strap properly, and was in the act of doing so when the Jawa seized. What really happened nobody will ever know for certain. At first, it was thought that Bill lost his life through head injuries which would not have occurred if his helmet had stayed on, but the German doctors told Mrs Ivy that if he hadn't died from his head injuries he would have died from the injuries to his chest. The doctors did everything they could, to no avail, for the damage to that courageous little body was irrepairable. Bill Ivy had ridden his last race.

Saturday July 12, 1969, was a black day for motorcycling. Never has the death of a rider had such an impact on the sport. The shock and the grief shared by thousands of enthusiasts the world over was made the more acute because their little idol had died through no fault of his own. He was a complete victim of circumstances, over which he had had no control.

Ivy's team-mate, Franta Stastny, withdrew from the East German Grand Prix as a mark of respect, and on race day, a floral tribute of red carnations was laid on the space Ivy would have occupied on the starting grid of the 350cc race. There was a one-minute's silence before the race, which Agostini won, and afterwards the Italian declared: 'This race I win not for Italy, but for Bill Ivy.' Over a year later, when he was interviewed, Giacomo still couldn't bear to talk or think about that fateful day. He said, 'Bill crashed just in front of me – it was a terrible, terrible day. I don't want to remember it.'

Whether Bill really did have a premonition about his death, who can tell? But the fact remains that he definitely sensed that the immediate future held something tragic for him. Disturbing and sad though it may be, several factors suggest that he had an insight into what fate held in store, yet he still carried on racing. He once told a woman who lived in the same block of flats, 'Racing is all right – but you never know when your number's coming up.' Thinking he was joking, she replied, 'Well, surely that's one of the things you don't think about, isn't it?' And Bill said, 'I suppose so, *but one of these days I won't be coming back!*'

Also, prior to his last trip abroad, Bill did the unprecedented thing of getting all his affairs in order. He attended to all his business, his paperwork, and tidied-up his flat meticulously. Furthermore, he left a sum of money with a friend and said, 'This is to pay for a booze-up for the boys if anything should ever happen to me, because I've got a feeling that one of these days I shan't be coming back.'

Several months before he died, Bill announced his intentions of writing his own book. He wasn't prepared to have it ghosted – he was going to do it himself. More than anything he wanted to publish all the details of his personal feud with Phil Read. He wanted the public to know the full story of all the controversy. Several people are under the impression that Bill actually started writing the book, but although intense searches have been made the manuscript has not been found, if it ever existed. One thing is certain; if Bill had written his own story it would have made tremendous reading, and in comparison this book is probably a poor substitute. Writing it has been a tremendous task, but I have enjoyed it, although I only wish that the circumstances could have been different, and that instead I had been just giving Bill a helping hand with his autobiography. Often, I have wondered what his opinion would be on what I have written about him, and sometimes I have almost felt that he was standing behind me, looking over my shoulder as I typed. I could hear him saying, 'Oi . . . come off it . . . that wasn't *quite* me!' Or, 'No, it wasn't like that at all. . . .'

Tragically, Bill was destined to die living the life he loved, and he left a gap in the racing world that could never be filled. With his passing a lot of the humour went out of the paddock, for such characters are a rarity. A trend-setter with a flamboyant image, a good sense of humour, immense courage, and a fiery tenacity which enabled him to extract the very best out of anything on wheels at speed. Bill achieved all his ambitions in motorcycling; he wanted to be successful, a professional; he wanted to become a works rider; he set his sights on winning the 125 and 500cc British Championships; being King of Brands, winning a TT, and ultimately becoming a world champion. All this he did. Shortly after he started motor racing, he told his mother, 'I think I'm going to make it.' And he would have done, too. Ivy climbed into the book of fame with some brilliant performances – his 125cc lap record at over 100 mph in the Isle of Man will probably stand for all time – but as much as anything he will be remembered for his personality by those who were privileged enough to have seen and met him.

As the memories of the past live on, the stopwatches will continue to click, the chequered flags will wave and the wheels of racing will write further chapters for the record books. New champions will topple the established aces from the pinnacles of fame until they, too, are forced down by youth and superiority. . . . But never again will there be another quite like Little Bill Ivy, the 'Just William' of the racing world . . . the fastest 63 inches on Earth.

Epilogue

ROY FRANCIS had been driving to Geoff Monty's garage to prepare his racing bikes for another meeting when the first news of Bill's accident came over the car radio. He was very concerned, but he knew how tough his little friend was. 'He'll pull through OK,' Roy told himself. He was busy working on his bikes with an ear cocked to the radio in the workshop when the second report came over. 'I was absolutely shattered when I heard Bill had died,' said Roy. 'I just couldn't believe it. I threw the spanners down and packed up racing there and then. I walked out, got in the car and just drove home. It was as if I was in some sort of bad dream.' Roy never went back to racing again, even though he was on the verge of establishing himself. Not because he was a coward or afraid for himself, but as he said, 'When Bill got killed there just didn't seem to be any point in riding any more – I just lost all interest.'

Bill Ivy's death stunned both the car and the motorcycle world and left a gulf in both spheres of racing and universal sadness. Letters of condolence and floral tributes poured in from all over the world and the tiny church was packed with racing people and fans who went to say farewell to little Bill as he took his last ride.

In less than six months Mrs Ivy had lost her husband and her only son, but she put on a courageous front which must have taken all the guts she could muster. In recognition of her son's services to the sport, Yamaha presented her with a 350cc racing motorcycle, and a miniature golden temple inscribed: 'Bill Ivy – you will always be a winner, on the circuits as well as in our hearts'.

A few weeks after Bill's death, Mrs Ivy went to a race meeting at Brands Hatch. Both her daughters had tried to dissuade her from going, but it had made no difference. 'I had to go,' she explained afterwards. 'It was a silent way of saying "Thank you" to everyone who had been so understanding. I wanted them to see that I hadn't turned against them after losing Bill. I don't think I could have found so much comfort and understanding in any other sport.'

How many mothers would have reacted as Mrs Ivy did? Who could have blamed her if she had turned against motorcycling and racing, condemned the futility of it all, and wanted nothing to do with anything connected with it? But Mrs Ivy would not.

People soon forget, but the racing fraternity has never forgotten Bill Ivy's mother. At first, somebody would call or phone to make sure she was all right. Many of the racing lads visited her and were invited in for a cup of tea and a chat. One young lad hitch-hiked all the way from Austria, and arrived saturated and exhausted on Mrs Ivy's doorstep – he wanted to see Bill's grave. She made him take a hot bath, gave him some dry clothes, fed him, and then, in typical motherly fashion, packed him off to bed. It turned out that the boy hadn't slept for two whole days on his journey to England.

Most people expected Mrs Ivy to sell the Yamaha that had been presented to her, but she refused to do this. 'Gifts,' she said, 'are not for selling or giving away.' But what could she do with it? Her plucky answer earned the admiration of race fans everywhere. Bill's words had kept coming back to her, 'You must find an interest . . . you'll be very lonely now Ringo's gone, and when the racing season starts and I'll be away most of the time you'll be lonelier still . . . you must find something to occupy yourself. . . .' What better interest could she have than an involvement in the sport which had made her son famous? Mrs Ivy made up her mind to sponsor a rider on the machine.

Tom Kirby's advice was sought, and immediately he offered to adopt the role of team manager, assisting Mrs Ivy in an advisory capacity. Permission was granted from the Yamaha factory in Japan to enter the machine as an Ivy-Yamaha, and Rex Butcher, a good, consistent and safe rider, was selected to race the bike. Rex was ideal, for Mrs Ivy didn't want a rider who might have caused her anxiety by riding over his limits and falling off.

For two years, Rex rode for the Ivy team, which was run by the only woman sponsor in Europe, then at the end of 1971 he retired from racing and a new rider had to be found. Fortuitously, Uncle Tom had been coaxing along a promising youngster called Jim Harvey for two seasons. In Tom's opinion, Jim was now ready for some really competitive machinery, and as the Ivy-Yamaha was one of the best standard production racing machines in the world it was agreed that Jim would take over from Rex. Tom Kirby had groomed many novices into star riders, so it was very fitting that his latest protégé should be given the opportunity of giving Mrs Ivy the success she so richly deserved.

Since losing her own son, Mrs Ivy has been adopted as 'Mum' by hundreds of racing men who have given her their respect and admiration. Her role as sponsor has kept her busy, attending race meetings and social functions where she is fussed-over constantly by riders and officials. She has had a glittering trophy made in memory of Bill – a solid silver crash helmet with a huge ivy leaf engraved on the front – which is presented annually to the winner of a special series of Bill Ivy Challenge Races held at various circuits throughout the season.

'I'm glad I decided to take up sponsoring,' said the woman they rightly call Mother Courage. 'Nowadays I'm always doing something. I receive invitations to functions, I go to as many races as I can, the phone is always ringing, people call, and I never have time to feel lonely . . . or to think too much about the past.'

Index

WE ARE SURE YOU WILL ENJOY READING

A MAN CALLED MIKE
Christopher Hilton

A major biography of Mike Hailwood, Britain's multiple motorcycle world champion and, for a period, Formula 1 and endurance racing driver, who captured the hearts of all racing enthusiasts by his skill, courage, personality and outrageous sense of fun. If ever a motorsport figure deserved the distinction of 'larger than life', it was Hailwood, whose extrovert character and legendary talent are still fondly remembered more than a decade after his tragic death in a road accident. A deeply-researched and sensitive tribute which will appeal to motorcycling and motorsport enthusiasts alike.

256 pages, 228 x 152mm, 100 illus. Softbound.

ISBN 0 947981 92 6   **£9.99**

CLASSIC MOTORCYCLE ENGINES
Vic Willoughby

Author of several distinguished motorcycle books, Willoughby was awarded the Montagu Trophy for this detailed evaluation of road and racing engines which earned supreme reputations for innovation and quality. Illustrated with photos and technical drawings, it has become a standard work on the subject. The book features engines from manufacturers including Ducati, JHP, Jawa, Kawasaki, Moto Guzzi, Norton and many more.

144 pages, 273 x 215mm, 170 illus. Casebound.

ISBN 0 947981 10 1   **£14.95**